Give Them The Words

Improving Communication for Exceptional Kids:
•Feelings •Emotions •Learning Styles •Self-Awareness
•Parental Guidance

Kim Gallo M.S., CCC-SLP

To Alden, My First Kid-Teacher

Without You, I Wouldn't Be Me

By reading this document, the reader agrees that under no circumstances is the author responsible for any losses, direct or indirect, that are incurred as a result of the use of the information contained within this document, including, but not limited to, errors, omissions, or inaccuracies.

Table of Contents

Introduction

Have you ever had a word stuck at the tip of your tongue - something that makes perfect sense in your head but little to those around you? Or have you had this happen to someone you know? For me, it's safe to say that I've experienced both. From being flustered enough to only mouth "uhs" and "ahs" to being presented with children who would do the same.

Words are our tools of communication, but sometimes learning to use those tools effectively can be difficult for both children and adults. Development of language takes place at different times, and so does the correct use of language, irrespective of whether a child is neurotypical or neurodiverse. Having said that, children can display differences when it comes to learning and then using language. Struggling to convey one's feelings accurately can be a frustrating exercise, and this book addresses those hurdles specifically.

This book was written to break these barriers, to topple the wall between those who look for semblance and those able to provide, and to give insight into the many experiences of neurodivergent children and adolescents from a speech pathologist's point of view. Not only will this book provide you with information regarding the importance and effectiveness of words, but it will also broaden your mind on the very subject.

There is likely a selection of books available for you to choose from, so why pick mine? It is fair to claim that I have inside experience when it comes to dealing with neurodivergent children and adolescents—especially ones that find it hard to use their words. While earning a bachelor's degree in psychology in the late '90s, I worked alongside certified Behavior Analysts teaching young toddlers who were newly diagnosed with Autism. I then earned a BCaBA (Board Certified Associate Behavior Analyst Certification) in 2002 and a master's degree in Speech-Language Pathology (SLP) in 2004. In 2005, I earned my Certificate of Clinical Competence (CCC) and became Certified by the American Speech and Hearing Association (ASHA). I have worked in Early Intervention and K-12 schools, as well as in private practice with both children and young adults. I am the parent of two, one of which is a neurodivergent young adult.

I will take you on a journey into the world of communication. Neurodivergent individuals can have difficulties expressing themselves, which becomes frustrating. However, when taught how to do so, they can reach a point where they feel less overwhelmed and less restricted. Feelings go hand in hand with words in that without a word to attach to a feeling, communication is pretty challenging. Activities engaging our senses are also useful, as well as forms of non-verbal communication that can be transformed into conversations.

On the subject of senses, we will look at all eight of them. Yes, there are eight, which open the door to sensory overload, which I will explain in detail. One has to remember that autistic children respond differently to sensory activation. For instance, one child may be very fond of loud music, whereas another will find loud music uncomfortable and anxiety-inducing. The same goes for touch and the other senses. You will learn the differences, and the concept of dysregulation, which amounts to being out of sync and displaying either high or low levels of arousal. The next section is a lesson on managing situations to facilitate regulation. This section will include the zones of regulation model, which classifies sensory experiences and movement between zones.

Communication is divided into eight categories, much like the senses, but the difference is that the categories are back-and-forth stepping stones used when communicating. Think of it like tennis; there is back and forth, but not always the same shot. The struggles that autistic children have within the categories are highlighted, and as parents or teachers of autistic children, you will identify.

I will also take you through the different styles of language learning, as a detailed breakdown, and give you exercises that suit verbal learners or natural learners, for instance. As with anyone, some children prefer learning in groups, while others favor individual learning. This concept is explored, along with the concepts of Gestalt and analytical language learners, followed by a detailed section on echolalia, which is the repetition of words without context. This is a particularly interesting trait for some children, and I will show you some exercises that can be done to create context and improve on using words correctly in a situation.

Sign language as a tool to work towards understanding how to build communication skills that become verbal will be explained, as well as methods involving devices like manual communication boards and voice output records, among others.

There will be detailed information on Early Intervention (EI) programs and the legislation that provides for equal education opportunities. Education is not restricted to school, and I will show you how to set up your home and how to interact with your child and the rest of the family. As a parent of an autistic child, I understand the challenges that parents face, which are elaborated on. In addition, I will explain some methods of mitigating the stress involved in raising children, autistic or not.

I have included some stories from parents of autistic children, transcribed directly from videos, that readers will identify with. It is always good to know that there are others with which you can empathize, and this section is a great reminder of that. Emotional support structures are touched on, and I explain the ways in which parents can manage the transition into adolescence. One of the ways is to build self-esteem in our children and to let them know that neurodiversity is a strength.

We all have differences in opinion about social media, but I think we can agree that teenagers love it. This does not mean that using social media is free of its problems. You will find some statistics and recommendations based thereon as to limited screen time and social media use in general.

I finish off with non-verbal autism, including augmentative and alternative communication systems, strategies, and tools. Visual displays such as charts and social stories are discussed, as well as the development of emotional intelligence. When you reach the end of your read, you will have a broader understanding of just how and why words are so essential. Rest assured, it is safe to say that you'll be able to "give them the words."

Chapter 1

Words and Feelings

"Sticks and stones might break my bones, but words will never hurt me." This is an idiom that nobody really knows the origin of. However, unless you are a psychopath, you know that it is not true!

Words

One of the definitions, according to Merriam-Webster's dictionary, is "a speech sound or series of speech sounds that symbolizes and communicates a meaning usually without being divisible into smaller units capable of independent use" (Merriam-Webster, n.d.). Words are important because they allow us to communicate our thoughts and feelings. Words can be spoken, written, or read. Words are powerful because they have the ability to make things happen. We use words to inform, confirm, deny, protest, negate, and question. Words are symbols that represent things and can also be represented visually, such as in drawings or photographs.

We can do so much with our words. Words provide affirmations of our thoughts. Words are powerful and can be used to cause pain or warm hearts. One single word can cause tremendous pain or give us hope. Words can also be empty. Have you ever had a conversation with someone who continues to talk incessantly regardless of whether you look or seem interested? They keep talking even when you are attempting to indicate that you are not following the story. Words can be deceptive. Misleading words, more commonly known as lies, are often spoken for a variety of reasons, such as to avoid punishment, to protect ourselves, to maintain our privacy, or to avoid embarrassment.

Words can be clues that are used to predict behavior. Words tell us a lot about one's character if we listen carefully. Words allow us to show how innovative, creative, and intelligent our minds can be. They can inspire and change our lives. Mental health workers, counselors, and teachers are just some professions with such immense power. A simple conversation with them can change a life forever.

On the other hand, negative, hurtful words impact people on a physical level. Has anyone ever used words that made you feel like you've been physically punched or stabbed? We must remember here that, of course, we cannot control what comes out of other people's minds and mouths, but we can choose to think about them in a way that leaves us feeling less wounded.

When we hear words from specific sources, it is natural for us to believe those words. Words spoken by familiar sources hold even more true when we hear the exact words repeatedly. Marketers and advertisers know that if you are exposed to a message frequently, you are more likely to believe it even when it contains a non-fact. People with low self-esteem often have low self-esteem because they've lived in a world created by someone else's words. One of the top thinkers on the future of culture, relevance, and the internet is Gary Vaynerchuk; he says:

"The number one way to protect a child is to build their self-esteem. When a child is not insecure, they don't succumb to danger" (Vaynerchuk, 2022). By using the right words, we can accomplish this.

As a Speech-Language Pathologist who works in a school setting with teens, I often have students come to my office for their therapy time. A while ago, I had a student come in, and while we were making our initial small talk, I noticed that he had an odd look. Initially, I just asked him if everything was okay, and he responded by saying, "I'm fine," but as I continued to talk, I felt like his face was trying to tell me something. I stopped talking and said to him, "Aiden (not his real name), I can tell by looking at your face that something is bothering you. Please tell me what's bothering you?" Initially, he said, "I feel like my brain is on crack." Still unclear on what that meant, I proceeded to ask him several more questions. He explained to me that there was a substitute teacher in the class that he had just come from. I was aware that youngsters in many schools don't always act in an appropriate manner when a replacement teacher is there. This substitute teacher was given a lesson plan and attempted to implement it. Unfortunately, the students had other ideas. Aiden explained that they were rambunctious, rowdy, and loud. They were out of their seats and ignored all the teacher's requests to sit and attend the lesson. Aiden was especially appalled that this adult female teacher could somehow tune out or ignore what she was witnessing. The substitute stood in front of the class and continued to try to teach the lesson even though only a handful of students were actually listening and ready to learn.

Aiden is a kind and thoughtful child. He is a diligent student and a conscientious worker. He is also Autistic. He and I proceeded to talk about what was happening inside of him while he was witnessing this madness. He explained to me, after a lot of coaxing, that at first, he was feeling a bit bothered, but it quickly turned into feeling confused and agitated about being in that classroom. He said, "My heart was beating fast for no reason, and I felt a little dizzy."

This child is an honor student with straight A's who receives positive teacher praise and prides himself in doing the right thing. He has friends and belongs to some of the school clubs. So, how could a child of his academic caliber and good senses not find the words to describe what he was experiencing during that class? And why didn't he just ask to be excused so he could get some air and relax? He didn't have the words.

I spent the rest of the session GIVING HIM THE WORDS.

Feelings

Learning to recognize our own thoughts and emotions is a skill that is crucial for children and adults to develop in order to be fully present in our lives. When we are unable to recognize our thoughts and feelings, it can lead to a wide range of behaviors, some of which may or may not be beneficial to our health. Abuse of substances like drugs and alcohol are common Band-aids used to alleviate suffering. The illusion of comfort can also be created by addictions such as compulsive overeating, gambling, or excessive exercise. Some people have the good fortune to discover more constructive strategies to deal with unsettling feelings. For instance, activities involving some form of art, such as dance or painting, provide a more constructive outlet for coping with uncomfortable feelings.

Whenever I consider how vital it is to pin down my emotions, music is the first thing that comes to me. If songwriters are confronted with powerful and overpowering sensations, they express those emotions through the lyrics of the songs they write. People have a lot on their plates because life can be difficult. Unanticipated events can occur at any time, and how we feel about them and how we respond to them are important factors in determining whether, how, when, and where we progress. When everything in the life of a healthy and balanced individual is going well, recognizing one's emotional space does not provide much of a challenge. We make it a habit to check in with ourselves periodically to ascertain how we feel and what we might require. Talking to someone who works in the field of mental health professions **and** who has received specialized training is a different experience than having that conversation with one of your closest friends or relatives. They utilize a variety of methods that will enable you to investigate your past and get a glimpse into your unconscious mind.

Regrettably, not everyone possesses the expertise, access, or finances necessary to collaborate with professionals such as these. Without a trained professional, such as a psychologist, how can you learn to recognize your feelings, find a solution to a problem, pull yourself out of a state of depression, or mend a broken relationship?

Dr. Joan Cusack Handler, author of the book "Identifying Your Feelings," is a psychologist and researcher. According to an article published in Psychology Today, we should "Start by taking our emotional temperature." She challenges us to identify the sensations that we are currently conscious of (Agnionline, n.d.). Which of the five senses predominates the most? And at what point did we first become conscious of the sensation? Next, what factors might contribute to producing this sensation? What is taking place in our everyday lives, and what is not taking place? If, at that time, we are unable to determine how we are feeling, she proposes that we evaluate our conduct and everyday life by questioning our home life, relationship with a partner, children, parents, and siblings, and other aspects of these relationships. Can you fill us in on the situation at work? Is one able to have fun there? Is everything all right with the manager? After you have provided your responses to these questions, you should consider the veracity of the answers you have provided. When you acknowledge an emotion, you can better understand what you're experiencing and why. It is also a test of how effectively you can understand the thoughts and feelings of other people. Having a skill as priceless and valuable as this one is hard to come by.

The majority of human communication is done through non-verbal means. It is essential to not only pay attention to the words being said but also be aware of what you may be seeing, as nonverbal cues such as facial expressions, vocal tone, and body language can frequently reveal how a person is feeling. It is essential for us to be human so that we are able to comprehend our own ideas and feelings (versus animals). When we have an understanding of our own thoughts and feelings, it will be easier for us to articulate why we feel the way we do and to empathize with the emotions that others are experiencing.

When we are able to verbally convey our thoughts, feelings, and experiences in the form of language, we are able to fulfill not just our own needs but also the needs of those around us. Your capacity to deal with an emotion is improved simply by being able to put a name to what you are experiencing and how you are feeling. The more words we provide children to describe their feelings and emotions, the more likely it is that they will acquire those words and be able to assimilate the important life lesson that it is highly beneficial and empowering to communicate our feelings and emotions. Because doing so requires a certain degree of openness and vulnerability, putting one's thoughts and feelings into words can be a challenging task.

We demonstrate our emotional intelligence and awareness when we are able to comprehend and think about how others feel, as well as when we are able to understand and think about how we ourselves feel. If we put that knowledge and attention to work to solve problems and take control of our feelings, we will be able to assist others in doing the same. Putting a name to an emotion makes it easier to manage and come to terms with that sensation.

One of the many meanings of the word "regulate" is "the ability to govern something, particularly by causing it to function in a predetermined manner," which can be found in the dictionary published by Merriam-Webster. There are many different kinds of regulations, and one of them is the regulation of emotions. This refers to our capacity to translate how we are feeling and what we are thinking into behaviors that are appropriate for the context in which we find ourselves. A person who possesses a high level of emotional intelligence has the ability to lessen the impact of strong feelings. They have the ability to adjust and reduce their levels of rage and anxiety.

The way one thinks has the power to alter the tone of what a person is feeling on the inside as well as on the outer. Even while most people are familiar with terms such as mad, sad, happy, excited, and angry, there are literally hundreds of more words that can be used to express feelings and emotions. Marc Brackett, the founder of the Yale Centre for Emotional Intelligence and influential psychologist, authored a book called Permission to Feel, in which he writes, "being able to communicate words such as shame, guilt, humiliation, jealousy, envy, joy, contentment, stress, and pressure displays some of the greatest levels of what is known as emotional intelligence" (Rabbitt, 2022). Think about how much more specific you are as a communicator when you describe someone or something by using terms like fulfilled, harmonic, and invigorated.

Chapter 2

The Eight Senses and Why They Really Matter

Our sensory system helps us get information about the world around us. The senses help us stay alive and well. They help us in everyday life, like playing sports, driving, or navigating an unfamiliar place. The senses help us when listening to a tune or enjoying a meal. The senses allow us to have enjoyable experiences. Our feelings, emotions, and memories are quite connected with the senses.

Looking back at my University days, training as a Speech-Language Pathologist in the early 2000s, I don't remember the sensory system being mentioned in the way I have come to know it.

In 2005, I began working on a multidisciplinary team of pediatric therapists. While there, I was introduced to play therapists, feeding specialists, and physical and occupational therapists. Some of these men and women would be working with the same children I was assigned to treat for a speech or language delay, difference, or disorder. At this facility, working among these professionals, I gained substantial insight and knowledge about the senses. When working with children under age six, I sometimes used a small, child-size table and chairs in my office when I wasn't sitting on the floor or using the playroom. One day, when working with a student, the Occupational Therapist (OT) walked into my workspace to grab a book. She looked at me and asked me, "Why are her feet dangling like that?" I thought the chair was small enough for a child under age six. Admittedly, it was slightly bigger than I'd like-but, just slightly more prominent. I looked up at the OT, feeling quite confused, not knowing what to say. Finally, she said, "You should put her feet up on some sort of box." Still confused and clueless, I replied, "I'm working on her speech development; what do her feet being on a box have to do with her ability to produce speech and language?." She answered my question, and I was intrigued by her unexpected and thorough answer. This was the start of MY Special Education as an SLP. For the next five years, I worked side-by-side with the "Dream Team." These were some of the kindest, most caring, and most intelligent women in the field. Together, we co-treated children while educating each other about the knowledge we had specific to our disciplines.

The most valuable lesson I have learned from this team is that all behavior is communication. I learned that most symptoms of behaviors we see in our children start in the nervous system. Admittedly, upon first hearing it, the terminology used by these therapists sounded "hokey" to me. They used all kinds of words and phrases I was unfamiliar with to explain things I perceived as moodiness, tantrums, or non-compliance. Several words I heard regularly that initially didn't make sense to me. Words like REGULATE, SENSORY DIET, VESTIBULAR INPUT, AND POOR PROPRIOCEPTION PROCESSING... What the heck kind of language was this? As I stated previously, this was the education I never knew I wanted, but I quickly realized it was the education I needed. And I didn't need it just to work with my Speech and Language students; I needed it for myself and my own child, who, luckily, was young enough at the time to benefit from all this crucial information. In order to explain what I've learned, I will start by building on some of the knowledge you most likely already have. We formally learn the basics of the five senses as young as kindergarten. By the time we get to a high school anatomy class, we can have a pretty detailed understanding of it. To refresh the memory of those who may have forgotten, the five senses are:

1. Olfactory/Smell: How something smells can help us know about the world. Smell is one of the principal ways we interact with the environment. Our sense of smell can be valuable in determining whether the milk is spoiled, or you are tracking dog feces throughout the house on the bottom of your shoe.

2. Vision/Sight Perception: Our eyes give us vital information about the world. Our sense of vision helps us see things that are near and

far. It helps us to detect light and color via the cells in the retina at the back of the eye.

3. Taste/Gustatory: Our tongue receives taste sensations and determines if the sensation is harmful. What we think about the flavor depends on combining our senses of taste, smell, and touch. The combination of these things determines whether we like the taste of food.

4. Touch/Tactile: There are nerve endings and touch receptors in the skin; this allows us to feel different textures, temperatures, and pain, which is necessary for avoiding injury.

5. Hearing/Auditory: The mechanical sense of hearing works by turning physical movement into electrical signals, which get translated into vibrations, and we experience those vibrations as sounds.

There are three more senses that are super significant. They are what I like to call the VIP Systems because they are Very Important Parts. They are as follows:

1. Vestibular Sense controls your balance and knowledge of where your body is in space.

2. Interoception is awareness of the body's physical signs and symptoms. It is what's happening inside the body and our attention to it. Are we hungry? Are we thirsty? Do we

have to urinate or have a bowel movement? Are we feeling chilly or too hot?

3. Proprioception Processing - this is the body's ability to sense itself. The body can vary how muscles, tendons, and joints respond to incoming information regarding outside forces.

Before I go on, I'd like to define a few words or terms that will hopefully help you understand what took me a while to figure out.

First, the Nervous system is the command center of the body (so it's super important that it works appropriately). It has four parts, as follows:

1. The Central Nervous System (CNS): The brain and the spinal cord

2. The Peripheral Nervous System (PNS): The nerves that connect the brain and spinal cord to the peripheral nervous system, which is what nerve tissue outside of the central nervous system is called.

3. Somatic Nervous System (SNS): Also part of the peripheral nervous system. One of its roles is to relay information we see, hear, and feel to the brain. It is responsible for the voluntary control of body movements. So, when we are thinking about walking, the SNS takes that thought, sends it to the muscles in our legs, and makes it happen. When

someone has a spinal cord injury, the messages cannot travel from the brain to the body. The spinal nerves below the injury level receive the signal but cannot travel up the spinal tract to the brain. One might continue to have reflex movements, but they are not purposeful or controllable.

4. The Autonomic System (ANS): One of the primary functions of the peripheral nervous system's autonomic nervous system, which controls glands and organs without the intervention of our conscious minds, is to maintain bodily functions.

Sympathetic and Parasympathetic Systems

These systems work together to coordinate the changes that our bodies require to function throughout the environment. For example, the pupils in our eyes adjust in size according to the light present to give us the best vision. Likewise, when the temperature gets hot, our sweat glands are turned on to regulate our body's internal temperature.

I like to think of the word regulate as regular. When you feel regular, you feel okay; you are not agitated or annoyed; you are not hot or hungry. When we hear the word sensory, just know we are referring to one of the senses. The term sensory dysregulation is used to describe someone whose body is over or under-reacting to the incoming sensory information.

We would then say that that person is poorly regulated.

What Does Poor Regulation Look Like? And What Kinds of Things Can Make Someone Dysregulated?

It can look like whining, tantrums, fussing, unsettled, highly emotional, or moody. The term level of arousal can be defined by how near or far a person is from being regular... oops, I meant regulated. Our ability to control our level of arousal is called self-regulation.

In a case of low arousal levels, it can look like the person is tired, lazy, or distracted. For example, a child may slump in their chair, need to prop their head up with their hands and become easily distracted by other sensory input in the room.

Children subject to high-level arousal may be in constant motion or appear agitated or disorganized. For example, a child may be bouncing, constantly getting out of their chair, climbing, or moving heavy objects around (like the sofa).

How Can an Adult, Parent, or Child Change the Arousal Level?

Sensory modulation: Helping and advising people to control their emotional state by employing their senses, such as sight, sound, smell, touch, taste, and movement. Some tools that can be used as examples are music, essential oils, rocking chairs, weighted items, and massage chairs. An optimum level of arousal is reached when the information your senses take in is tolerable and allows you to function well.

What Does This Look Like in an Actual Situation Regarding a Child?

Jayden is a 7-year-old 1st-grade student at Mariner Elementary School. He loves wearing sweatpants because they are soft and comfortable. He wakes up one morning and begins getting ready for the day. Unfortunately, his mom got behind on the laundry, so the only clean thing he can wear is jeans. So, his mom helps him put on the jeans while he attempts to wiggle away from her. Because of the jeans, Jayden's nervous system is activated. Jayden goes downstairs to eat breakfast. Mom serves Rice Krispies versus the Corn Flakes that Jayden usually prefers. He has some oral hypersensitivity, which causes him to choose a dry crunchy texture versus a soft mushy one. When the milk hits the Krispies, they get way too soggy. Now Jayden is getting even more dysregulated. Mom can't drive Jayden to school that day because she has an appointment, so she asks Pam, the neighbor, to take him. Unfortunately for Jayden, neighbor Pam has two 4th-grade rambunctious twins, and Jayden has a sensitive hearing auditory system. Now he's on his way to school, and the other children are playing around. The twins are inadvertently touching him, and their voices are loud. This adds another couple of notches to his already dysregulated nervous system. He finally arrives at school, and another child takes off his backpack, and his arm accidentally touches Jayden's shoulder. Jayden loses the ability to control himself and punches the child. His school day hasn't even started, and he is already at the top of the chart with every sensory event that challenges his nervous system. This sensory overload or high dysregulation activated his sympathetic nervous system and pushed him into a fight, flight, or freeze mode. While there are several techniques to de-escalate this response, prevention of the build-up of several sensory events is what's ideal.

As educators, we must do all that we can to prevent this from happening to our children because, over time, the consequences of this chronic stress can lead to other mental and physical problems, such as anxiety and depression, as well as physical challenges such as high blood pressure and hair loss.

As a parent, addressing your own nervous system is important because mirror neurons fire when we are experiencing something and when we witness someone experiencing something. Our children are mirroring our nervous system, and we are mirroring their nervous system. So, parents have to learn how to REGULATE their own nervous system so they can be in an ideal position to help their children.

Sensory Dysregulation in More Detail

According to Sydney Thorson, OT, "sensory dysregulation refers to a mind or body state which occurs when the body is out of balance due to experiences in the sensory environment" (Thorson, 2022). When we experience things through our senses, those stimuli make us feel a certain way. My tolerance for music at volume 10 is different from my son's. I have tolerance for the tag on my shirt-my daughter will lose her mind if it touches her neck and back. I can eat lunch at a table with my peers; a co-worker, Mr. Jones, smells my yogurt and begins to gag. Sensory dysregulation happens when the body's nervous system perceives too much or too little stimulation for best functioning, and self-regulation is not naturally occurring. I had a toddler-age student years ago when I was working for Early Intervention, whose body was always in motion. He had a strong, solid build. He was an agile climber and was quite tolerant of pain. He rarely cried when he had a fall that resulted in him being bruised or bloodied. He stuffed large quantities of food in his mouth when self-feeding. His mother was often worried he would choke. After working with the "Dream Team," I knew this child was a sensory seeker. His nervous system was understimulated, so his body spent much of its time seeking ways to self-regulate.

Everyone's nervous system is different. Everyone's ability to self-regulate is also different. When you are in tune with what your body needs when something is too much or too little, you can simply adjust your choices or the environment. Sometimes our children present undesired behaviors that we often don't understand. There is a strong possibility that the issue may be stemming from their nervous system.

Contrary to what many people believe, your child will not grow out of their sensory issues. No amount of discipline will change how a child's body feels when it's not regulated. Children often act out because they feel overwhelmed or unsafe. Things like timeouts and punishment do not improve those conditions. If your child climbs all over the furniture and jumps on their bed, it could be happening because their sensory system requires an increased need for movement. If your child is clingy and it seems as though they have to touch everything in the environment, they may be struggling with body awareness and may not even realize exactly where their body is in relation to yours.

Simply put, when the nervous system isn't balanced, it can be due to a condition called Sensory Processing Disorder (SPD). Children and adults with SPD feel dysregulated more often than neurotypicals. Without intervention, they have far less ability to self-regulate. While SPDs can exist in isolation, they may be most prevalent in those with Autism Spectrum or Attention Deficit Disorders.

How can we help? How can Jayden's before-school scenario look brighter moving forward? When children are struggling to modulate their senses, and as a result, negative consequences occur. I recommend consulting an occupational therapist or developmental pediatrician. First, as parents, we can learn to track the triggers. We need to explore how different sensations make our children feel. Certain places, bright light, loud noises, and not knowing what will happen next are all things that can be too much or not enough for some children. Getting wet, getting dirty, going for car rides, being interrupted while talking, or making a mistake can also produce an unexpected response from a child. After experiencing some of the circumstances I just mentioned, it can make a child feel anywhere in the range between feeling nothing at all or they may feel unbearable. Some signs that your child may be experiencing sensory overload include touching everything, running or pacing, jumping on the furniture, covering their ears, squinting their eyes are blinking, rolling on the floor, making noises, often complaining that things are too loud, too bright too tight, chewing on things that are not necessarily edible, and poor eye contact. In the case of Jayden, he was experiencing higher and higher levels of arousal as the morning progressed. When he got to school, his nervous system was overloaded, and he lost control. He would benefit from an occupational therapy evaluation and treatment plan.

Occupational therapists often recommend "sensory diets" to children with self-regulation challenges. The term "diet" initially confused me because I associate the word diet with food. However, a sensory diet is not necessarily about food. It is more like a plan, recommended to regulate (calm or arouse) depending on the affected senses. We must be willing to experiment and make changes.

We can use devices in each sensory-system category to stimulate or calm the nervous system. The same device, such as a swing, may calm one child and may trigger another child. The tool can have no effect at all, or it can relax, excite, or trigger. Here are some explanations and examples:

Touch/Tactile

Sensory seekers crave touch, generally have a high tolerance for pain, and often get messy. Sensory avoiders avoid touch, prefer certain textures, are very neat, and start away from crowds. The following sensory supporting devices can be used:

- bins filled with rice

- weighted blankets and vests

- firm squeezes

- playdough moon sand

Sight/Visual

Seekers will stare at ceiling fans or lights, hold items very close to their eyes, and lose their places while reading. Avoiders dislike bright light, struggle with eye contact, and are startled easily. The following sensory supporting devices can be used:

- light table

- lava lamps or something similar

- marbles

Hearing/Auditory

Seekers tend to make loud noises, have the TV volume up high, and use such to feel calm. Avoiders don't like crowds, will often be seen covering their ears, and do not like everyday sounds (blender or a flushing toilet). The following sensory supporting devices can be used:

- quiet space

- earplugs or headphones

- calming music

- learning a musical instrument

Taste/Oral

Seekers enjoy strong tastes like spicy foods and will often chew on non-edibles. Avoiders stay away from certain textures of foods and are very restricted in what they eat, and may find it difficult to use some utensils (knives, forks, cups, straws). The following sensory supporting devices can be used:

- chewing gum or eating candy

- chewable toys or jewelry

- blowing whistles, horns, and bubbles

- trying new foods

- trying utensils made of novel materials

- using a vibrating toothbrush

Smell/Olfactory

Seekers tend to smell objects but also people. They find strong smells appealing and actively seek them out. Avoiders can find ordinarily pleasant smells very unpleasant. The following sensory supporting devices can be used:

- scented toys or playdough

- aromatherapy

- perfumes or cologne

- strongly scented objects stored away

Vestibular

The vestibular system doesn't affect seeking and avoiding behavior but rather affects spatial awareness, coordination, and balance. Sport, especially involving a ball, has shown to be effective in improving the aforesaid skills. The following sensory supporting devices can be used:

- swinging

- bike riding

- swimming

- playing catch

- kicking a soccer ball

Interoception

Interoception allows individuals to perceive the internal state of their own body, including sensations such as hunger, thirst, heart rate, breathing rate, and temperature interoception plays a critical role in regulating the body's internal processes and maintaining homeostasis and is also thought to be involved in emotional and social cognition, as well as decision-making and self-awareness. Individuals with impaired interoception may experience difficulties in recognizing and responding to their own bodily needs and emotions.

The interception system struggles to provide an identification of cold, warmth, thirst, or hunger. Teaching children about their bodies improves awareness of what they are experiencing. The best way to do so is to increase awareness by saying something such as, "It's been four to five hours since you last ate something. You are likely feeling hungry." Then have the child gain awareness of how they are feeling at that moment. This is a complicated sense, and for those who struggle with it, a more systematic guide may be required. In the interoception curriculum, author Kelly Mahler outlines an approach professionals can use to teach parents and clients.

Proprioception

Proprioception is the sense that allows individuals to perceive the position and movement of their own body without relying on visual or auditory cues. This sense is made possible by specialized receptors located in muscles, tendons, and joints that send information to the brain about the body's position, tension, and movement. Proprioception plays a critical role in movement control, balance, and coordination and is essential for a wide range of activities, from simple tasks like walking and grasping objects to complex activities like playing sports and performing dance routines.

Fine motor skills and their operation fall under proprioception and the associated difficulties. Random arm and leg movements are a result of the brain's proprioceptive communication in children. Muscle control can also be challenging, meaning that children may exert too much force without realizing it. The following sensory supporting devices can be used:

- Creating an obstacle course at home.

- Throwing a tennis ball back and forth.

- Lifting and replacing heavy objects.

- Jumping on trampolines.

- Massages involving different levels of pressure.

Learning the words that are associated with the feelings and sensitivities will help you better understand your child or student and their struggles and emotions. The words we use to communicate with them can be harmful or helpful. Speak respectfully to your children. Your words can show that you value them and will eventually become the words they hear in their heads (self-talk). If we want to teach boundaries, expectations, and consequences, our goal is to do it by talking in such a way that they learn something but do not feel afraid, belittled, or stupid.

Consider the following options:

- Calm down, versus I see you are having a hard time.

- It's no big deal. It's just a fire truck versus if you need to cover your ears, that's okay.

- Big boys can sit through a haircut versus I understand it's hard for you. Let's take a break.

If we stop and think about how paramount it is to have a regulated and balanced nervous system, we may realize how in vain some of the things we've been trying to teach our children have been. Teaching social skills and improving executive function are areas of difficulty for many children and adults with Autism and ADHD. Parents and educators often attempt to improve these skills as it is often blatantly apparent that they are areas of need. However, our ability to make gains in those areas may not be entirely possible if our level of arousal is not ideal. The emotions that go along with anxiety or anger can shut down one's awareness and ability to process what's going on around them. Those mirror neurons mentioned earlier in this chapter are visible in MRI studies. They are believed to be required to learn and apply social skills. Although they are visible, they have not turned on because the body isn't regulated. The lack of organizational skills that is a struggle for so many children is much more possible when the body isn't in a constant state of unbalanced arousal.

The Zones of Regulation

Leah Kuypers, the creator of the Zones of Regulation curriculum, is an OT who specializes in social learning and self-regulation. She is a graduate of both the University of Wisconsin-Madison and the University of St. Paul, with vast experience in her field. Kuypers' motivation for creating the curriculum came from her observations of the difficulties that her students had with regulation and emotional control (Kuypers, 2014). She describes the curriculum as follows:

A systematic, cognitive-behavioral approach is used to teach us how to regulate our feelings, energy, and sensory needs in order to meet the demands of the situation around us and be successful socially.

There are four zones, which are determined by feelings and current state, into which autistic children fit, depending on outside factors. Each zone is comparable to traffic signs and their meanings.

The Red Zone (Stop Sign)

Heightened states of alertness and intense emotions fit into this zone. For instance, terror, anger, devastation, or elation.

The Yellow Zone (Proceed With Caution)

The yellow zone is also associated with heightened emotions that lean towards the intense side. However, this zone occupies more control over feelings such as excitement, frustration, anxiety, or nervousness.

The Green Zone (Good to Go)

A calmer state of alertness is categorized by the green zone, which provides the best learning conditions. Emotions, such as happiness, focus, and willingness to be taught, are found within the green zone.

The Blue Zone (Rest and Re-energize)

The blue zone is used to describe low levels of alertness, like sadness or boredom.

Transitions Between Zones

We must remember that there is nothing wrong or abnormal about the emotional experiences in each zone. Still, it can be challenging to transition from one zone to the other. That is where the learning comes in. It is important to teach children to identify what zone they are occupying and how to manage that zone, taking into consideration the environment and circumstances.

Think back to your school days and the transition between the excitement and erratic nature of the playground to the calm and structured environment in the classroom. The yellow zone excitement, provided by playground activities, needs to transition into the calm focus of the green zone to best promote learning. That transition becomes easier if a child can identify which zone they are in and when to move to another zone, as is the goal of Leah Kuypers' curriculum.

Benefits

The zones are inclusionary for all neurodivergent children. Positive social and emotional learning is most often the result of the curriculum, and the language used during implementation is neutral and simple. Teachers, and the children being taught, continue to benefit mutually from the curriculum, which is a testament to its success.

Parents may find it beneficial to use the poster or printout of the zones (or something similar) at home. You can have it laminated and then attach photos of the child (which can be moved around on the chart) according to how they feel at a particular moment. This can be super helpful in putting feelings into pictures and words. When we know exactly what's going on with our children, we are better equipped to help them deal with things. They may need help figuring out how to feel more alert or de-escalate. They may need a break before they transition from one activity to the next, or they may fare better if we reduce the demands on them.

Chapter 3

Eight Parts of Communication

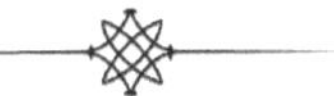

Humans are unique among all other species in the world in that they are self-conscious. We have some of the most sophisticated and nuanced forms of communication. People of all ages and from all walks of life must be able to effectively communicate if they are to survive. The process by which individuals of any species or civilization exchange thoughts, knowledge, emotions, details, and points of view with one another can be referred to as communication. A conversation may have a variety of objectives. The most frequent purpose, however, is to enable people who belong to the same species or civilization to understand one another better.

This is no different when it comes to neurodivergent children as well. These children and adolescents communicate for the same reason as everybody else does. There are a variety of reasons why neurodivergent children can have an especially hard time trying to put their thoughts into words. How can we help give them the words?

To better understand the complexity of communication, let's look at the several processes that are involved in carrying out a conversation. The communication process can be divided into eight crucial parts, each of which performs a vital role in the process as a whole:

- source

- message

- channel

- receiver

- feedback

- environment

- context

- interference

Source

The message is conceived by the source, which also produces and transmits it. The information is either presented to or sent to the audience (receiver) after the source has encoded it by selecting the precise sequence of words or the most appropriate phrases to communicate the intended meaning. The source can determine how effectively the audience has understood the message by monitoring the audience's response and then providing clarification or additional information.

Message

The stimulus or meaning that is created by the source for the receiver or audience is what is referred to as the message. The message is not just about the meaning that is communicated through the use of words but also about how the meaning is communicated through nonverbal cues, structure, grammar, style, and other components.

Channel

The channel can be thought of as the path that a message or messages take from the sender to the recipient. Face-to-face interactions, speeches, phone calls, voicemails, radio, public address systems, and Zoom are all examples of spoken channels. Letters, memos, purchase orders, invoices, articles published in newspapers and magazines, blogs, emails, text messages, tweets, and other forms of written communication are examples of written channels. It's also important to note that neurodivergent individuals may use multiple communication methods to convey a message, including spoken language, written language, and nonverbal communication, such as sign language and AAC. And even if an individual uses one communication method, it does not mean that it is the only one they understand. Therefore, it's important to be open and to use multiple forms of communication in order to facilitate effective communication with a neurodivergent person.

Receiver

The receiver takes the message from the source and then analyzes and interprets the message in a variety of ways, some of which the originator may not have intended. As a result, sometimes messages are misinterpreted by the listener. Some neurodivergent individuals may have difficulty processing verbal language, which can make it hard for them to understand spoken or written messages. There are multiple reasons why that may occur. Here are a few examples:

Difficulty With Social Cues

Many neurodivergent individuals may have difficulty interpreting nonverbal cues, such as facial expressions, body language, and tone of voice. This can make it hard for them to understand the intended meaning of a message.

Difficulty With Abstract Concepts

Some neurodivergent individuals may have difficulty understanding abstract concepts, such as sarcasm, idioms, and figurative language.

Limited Perspective-Taking

Some neurodivergent individuals may have difficulty understanding the perspective of others, which can make it hard for them to understand the intended meaning of a message.

Difficulty With Memory

Some neurodivergent individuals may have difficulty remembering and processing information, which can make it hard for them to understand and retain new information.

Limited or Specific Interest

Some neurodivergent individuals may have a limited or specific interest that could cause them to interpret information or messages in a specific way that is related to their interests.

It's important to note that neurodivergent individuals may all have different difficulties and strengths. Therefore, it's vital to be patient and flexible and to use multiple forms of communication in order to facilitate effective communication with a neurodivergent person.

Difficulty Understanding and Using Verbal Language

Some neurodivergent individuals may have difficulty processing verbal language, which can make it hard for them to understand spoken or written messages.

Difficulty With Social Cues

Many neurodivergent individuals may have difficulty interpreting nonverbal cues, such as facial expressions, body language, and tone of voice. This can make it hard for them to understand the intended meaning of a message.

Difficulty With Abstract Concepts

Some neurodivergent individuals may have difficulty understanding abstract concepts, such as sarcasm, idioms, and figurative language.

Limited Perspective-Taking

Some neurodivergent individuals may have difficulty understanding the perspective of others, which can make it hard for them to understand the intended meaning of a message.

Difficulty With Memory

Some neurodivergent individuals may have difficulty remembering and processing information, which can make it hard for them to understand and retain new information.

Visual/Spatial

The visual learner creates an image in their head that corresponds to what they have just learned. They favor the dissemination of information over a solitary writing approach that simply uses words. Students who major in spatial studies typically have highly developed senses of smell and hearing but have trouble listening to others.

Because spatial learners are visual by nature, they are adept at reading both people and situations by taking in the details of their surroundings, including body language and facial expressions.

It's important to note that different neurodivergent individuals may have different difficulties and strengths. Therefore, it's important to be patient and flexible and to use multiple forms of communication in order to facilitate effective communication with a neurodivergent person.

Feedback

You are providing feedback whenever you respond to the source, whether your response is purposeful or unintentional. The messages that are sent from the receiver back to the source are what make-up feedback. Whether verbal or nonverbal, all of these feedback signals enable the source to determine how successfully and accurately the message was received, as well as how poorly and inaccurately it was received.

Environment

The atmosphere, both physically and psychologically, in which you transmit and receive messages is referred to as the environment. Your environment, the people in it, animals, and even technology can all have an impact on how you communicate.

Context

The context of the communication contact includes the individuals engaged, the scenario they are in, and the environment in which they find themselves. Business attire is one example of the environmental cues that could be present in a professional communication setting. These cues can have a direct or indirect impact on the participants' expectations for language and behavior.

Interference

Interference, often known as noise, can originate from a variety of different sources. "Interference" refers to anything that gets in the way of or alters the meaning of the message that was intended by its source. This may be something exterior, or it may be something internal or psychological. The usual processes of encoding and decoding the message that is transmitted via the channel between the source and the receiver are disrupted by noise.

Chapter 4

Language Learning Styles

Everyone has their unique qualities, and this is something that rings especially true when it comes to the acquisition of any new talent. Languages included.

You might be familiar with or have heard material about the various learning styles and how it is possible to become a more effective language student by adapting your study methods to fit your unique learning style.

The reality, though, is that there is a great deal more nuance involved than that.

Study after study in the realm of science has come to the same conclusion: there is no clear answer. That is to say: It is not at all obvious whether adapting one's tactics for learning a language (or any learning strategy) to the most effective learning style would result in improved retention of the information that has been learned.

If one doesn't try to figure out which learning style one likes and instead just utilizes tactics that are tailored to that style, one might be able to obtain outcomes that are on par with those that they would get if they learned using a method that wasn't their natural inclination.

Your motivation will remain high, and the experience will continue to be enjoyable if you tailor your learning to focus more on your preferred learning method. It is not enough to just complete activities that are a perfect match for your unique method of learning. It's best to use a variety of approaches to education.

All of this is increasingly important when it comes to neurodivergent children learning a language. At times, acquiring the correct words can be a challenge for neurotypicals. Tailoring a neurodivergent child's learning experience to their preferred learning style will make them keener to continue learning and, as a result, reap far better rewards.

Let's take a look at different learning styles and some examples of them:

Visual or Spatial Learners

A visual learning style refers to how individuals learn and process information through visual cues, such as images, diagrams, videos, and other types of visual aids. Some examples of visual learning strategies include:

- Using flashcards to memorize information.

- Creating charts or diagrams to organize information.

- Drawing or sketching to understand new concepts.

- Using images or videos to supplement reading or lectures.

Some of the benefits of visual learning include:

- Enhancing memory retention.

- Creating a deeper understanding of concepts.

- Making learning more interactive.

- Engaging in improving problem-solving skills.

Spatial learning style refers to how individuals learn and process information through spatial cues, such as shapes, patterns, and visual-spatial relationships. Some examples of spatial learning strategies include:

- Using maps and graphs to understand information.

- Using mental imagery to recall information.

- Building 3D models to understand concepts.

- Playing spatial reasoning games.

Likewise, the benefits of spatial learning include:

- Improving spatial reasoning skills.

- Enhancing problem-solving abilities.

- Creating a deeper understanding of concepts.

- Enhancing memory retention.

Visual language learners do very well when they supplement their lessons with charts and color-code concepts in order to make the knowledge easier to remember. People who remember information better when it is presented in a visual format, such as a table, picture, graph, or presentation, are the best candidates for this type of learning style.

Visual learners sometimes struggle in traditional classrooms because of the excessive amount of information presented in a sequential fashion, but verbal and analytical learners flourish in these settings.

Consider the construction of a miniature airplane, for instance. Some children are able to put the puzzle together just by looking at the individual parts, while others require step-by-step visual directions. They are unable to participate in any activity unless they have a complete understanding of the situation.

For the same reason, people do not always pay attention to the details. Concepts are only retained in the memories of spatial learners when they are connected to other concepts or visualized in their minds.

Engaging in activities such as the arts, building blocks, video games, photography, architecture, or engineering are excellent choices for students who learn best through the use of their visual and spatial abilities.

It's important to note that people may have a preference for one or multiple learning styles. Also, some individuals may not have a preference for any particular learning style. Furthermore, people tend to use different learning strategies depending on the task or subject matter. Therefore, it's important to be open to different forms of learning and not to limit oneself to a single learning style.

Aural or Auditory Learners

Aural learning style refers to the way in which individuals learn and process information through sound and music. Some examples of aural learning strategies include:

- Listening to music or audio recordings to memorize information.

- Using mnemonic devices such as rhymes or songs to remember information.

- Listening to lectures or presentations.

The benefits of aural learning include:

- Enhancing memory retention.

- Creating a deeper understanding of concepts.

- Making learning more interactive and engaging.

- Improving problem-solving skills.

Auditory learning style refers to the way in which individuals learn and process information through verbal or spoken language. Some examples of auditory learning strategies include:

- Listening to lectures or presentations.

- Participating in group discussions.

- Reading aloud or recording oneself while studying.

- Using verbal cues or mnemonics to remember information.

The pros of the auditory learning style can include:

- Improving listening and verbal communication skills.

- Enhancing problem-solving abilities.

- Enhancing memory retention.

Aurals favor being told how to do something verbally rather than reading the instructions. They are articulate, have good recall, and are great at telling stories, explaining their ideas, speaking in public, and remembering knowledge. Additionally, they are very good at remembering information. You are most likely an auditory learner if you find that you are able to solve difficulties by talking about them out loud, even to yourself, and if you enjoy participating in study groups.

These pupils may benefit from traditional education because they have no problem following dictation and engaging in activities that need repetition. When it comes to acquiring a new language, students who learn best through aural means gain by practicing with a second person, recording their lessons, questioning their teachers, instructing others, and taking part in classroom debates.

Verbal or Linguistic Learners

Verbal learning style refers to how individuals learn and process information through the use of spoken or written language. Verbal learning strategies can include:

- Reading and writing to understand and retain information.

- Participating in group discussions and debates.

- Using verbal cues or mnemonics to remember information.

- Summarizing information in writing or verbally.

Verbal learning is particularly helpful in improving reading and writing skills, enhancing memory retention, and improving problem-solving skills.

Linguistic learning style refers to the way in which individuals learn and process information through the use of language and communication, such as verbal or written language. Still, it includes the study of language, grammar, vocabulary, and other linguistic elements. Linguistic learning strategies often include reading and writing to understand and retain information, studying grammar and vocabulary, participating in language learning classes, and analyzing literature.

Linguistic learning is beneficial for improving language skills, creating a deeper understanding of language and communication, and improving problem-solving skills.

Individuals who take pleasure in acquiring knowledge via the study of language in any of its forms can consider adopting the linguistic learning style. They are able to comprehend and recall an idea more easily when it is presented to them using wordplay, metaphors, analogies, and rhymes.

Words and expressions from their expanded vocabularies are easily retained by them and transformed into stuff that is immediately used in their thoughts. They are the ones who read the entire book even though their homework simply requires them to read the first chapter because they thrive on reading and writing exercises.

Verbal learners benefit tremendously by participating in role plays and group discussions. When a person is learning a second language, it is simple for them to recall words and idioms, link those words and idioms to other people, and finally express themselves using the new language.

Because they have an interest in literature, there is a good chance that they will begin reading for pleasure in their second language. This will both hasten their progress and make it easier for them to retain the material.

People who prefer to read books versus watching movies have a certain type of learning style that correlates to their preference. They are good listeners and have a tendency to do well on tests. They also keep journals, love tongue twisters, and learn new words.

Social Learning Style

Social learning style is the way in which individuals learn and process information through social interactions and interactions with others. Some examples of social learning strategies are:

- Collaborating with peers to solve problems or complete projects.

- Participating in group discussions and debates.

- Learning through mentorship or apprenticeship.

- Observing and imitating the behavior of others.

These strategies are helpful in:

- Improving communication and teamwork skills.

- Enhancing problem-solving abilities.

- Creating a deeper understanding of society.

- Building confidence and self-esteem.

- Creating opportunities for feedback and constructive criticism.

- Developing a sense of belonging and connectedness.

People who enjoy and get the most out of social engagement are characterized by this type of learning style. They learn valuable information via group conversations, group lessons, and collaboration that they participate in.

Social learners can flourish with the help of role-playing and question-and-answer sessions. They can easily read people, including interpreting their body language, tone of voice, and emotions displayed on their faces. This ability is referred to as "people smart." They may have difficulty completing their assignments and projects on their own, but they are eager to participate in class, ask questions, and make new friends.

Those who are social learners and study languages will benefit from having homework that entails conducting interviews with other people, collaborating with others, or attending group sessions. They would benefit from meeting new people and sharing their knowledge with others because it is both significant and beneficial to them.

Physical Learners

Physical learning style is the way in which individuals learn and process information through physical movement and hands-on activities. Some examples of physical learning strategies include:

- Using manipulatives or hands-on materials to understand and retain information.

- Engaging in movement or physical activity while studying.

- Using visual aids or diagrams to understand concepts.

- Using mnemonic devices that involve physical movement.

Benefits of physical learning include:

- Enhancing muscle-memory.

- Improving problem-solving skills.

- Making learning more interactive and engaging.

- Improving motor skills.

- Helping people to engage with the material in a more meaningful way.

Physical language learners flourish from physical contact and manipulating materials. Learners who benefit most from tactile experiences are those who profit from learning by doing and through hands-on activities such as sketching, playing with clay, working puzzles, dancing, modeling, and role-playing.

Online language instruction is beneficial for students who have a style of learning that is similar to this one. They find that studying on rocking chairs, chewing gum, and clicking pens is helpful. They find that writing things down helps them recall them better, but they have difficulty following instructions. The thought of being forced to sit motionlessly for long periods of time and having to concentrate for extended periods of time can feel like a nightmare.

Students who learn better through kinesthetic activities like making posters, going on field trips, conducting experiments, and creating collages are more likely to create diagrams, charts, and concept maps than auditory learners are.

Natural Learners

Natural learning is a style of learning that emphasizes the use of real-life experiences and hands-on activities to acquire knowledge and skills. It is based on the idea that people learn best when they are actively engaged in experiences that are relevant to their interests and needs.

Examples of natural learning include:

- Gardening and farming as a way to learn about botany and ecology.

- Cooking as a way to learn about nutrition and chemistry.

- Building and repairing as a way to learn about physics and engineering

- Traveling as a way to learn about different cultures and geography.

Benefits of natural learning include:

- Increased engagement and motivation as the learning is relevant and interesting to the learner

- Development of practical skills that can be immediately applied in real-life situations.

- Greater retention of information as the learning is reinforced through hands-on experiences.

- Development of a deeper understanding of the subject matter as the learner is able to make connections between the material and their own experiences.

Activities that require hands-on participation can also be beneficial for students who learn in a natural way. Lessons taught outside are empowering for students who are driven by their senses and who have a passion for nature, discovery, and investigation.

Natural learners would thrive in non-traditional educational environments like those provided by Montessori and other similar institutions. They tend to have an interest in animals, geology, the environment, and weather. Natural learners have an advantage in these fields because of their close connection to the natural world. They are able to conduct research, investigate subjects, and keep a diary about their discoveries when they are learning languages. In addition, many have the ability to generate writings about topics associated with biology, environmental news, and non-fiction literature.

Analytic Learners

Logical learning, also called analytical learning, refers to the style of learning that emphasizes the use of reasoning and critical thinking to acquire knowledge and skills. It is based on the idea that people learn best when they are presented with logical explanations and can see the connections between different concepts and ideas.

Links With Savants

This may seem like a bit of a tangent, but due to the literal and logical tendency of many autistic individuals, math skills can often be excellent. The Merriam-Webster definition of a savant is as follows:

A person affected with a developmental disorder (such as autism or intellectual disability) who exhibits exceptional skill or brilliance in some limited field (such as mathematics or music).

It makes sense that many autistic individuals are good at math. Interestingly, music is similar to math in that there is a specific formula that never changes. Take guitar, for instance. If you push down on a certain string and then pluck it, the sound will always be the same. If you then put your finger in a different place and pluck the string, the sound will be different from the first sound, but with that finger position, the sound will never differ from itself. Essentially both math and guitar/music are logical.

Further examples of logical learning include analyzing scientific experiments as a way to learn about cause-and-effect relationships. Debating is a way to learn about different perspectives and reasoning, which often doesn't come as easily as playing strategy games as a way to learn about problem-solving and logic.

Further benefits of logical learning include the development of critical thinking skills, which are valuable in many areas of life. Increased ability to understand and analyze complex information, greater understanding of the relationships between different concepts and ideas, and improved problem-solving skills, as the learner is able to break down and analyze problems logically. A stark benefit of this type of thinking and the application thereof is the adversity, probably sub-conscious to snap decisions. Contrast that with a bipolar individual in a manic phase, and decide what type of thinking would be more conducive to good decision-making. The answer is obvious.

The Framing Effect

We often see this in marketing and advertising. For example, you're looking for a dress, and you see two adverts:

1. Blue dress for sale at $75

2. Blue dress on sale at 50% off the usual price of $150

The illusion that most customers would succumb to is the perceived $75 saving, even though both offers have an identical purchase price. In the literal analytical and logical mind of an autistic individual, option 1 is the likely choice.

Analytical/Logical Learning

The analytical learning approach is excellent for quickly recognizing patterns and trends in any form of data. They never stop looking for the reasons or causes behind things, in addition to the consequences that can be shown objectively. The ability to interpret all of them, make logical inferences, and draw relationships is a strength of logical learners.

The learner who thinks analytically is fascinated by finding out how things function. Logic and structures fascinate them, and they take great pleasure in developing efficient, well-thought-out procedures for themselves and others.

They are masters in finding solutions to difficult problems and conundrums. You'll have no trouble recognizing them because they constantly question, "Why?" They have a natural tendency to reason and arrive at conclusions based on data. One of their major skills is their ability to memorize equations and information.

People who prefer material to be delivered sequentially and who prefer to tackle one challenge at a time are associated with this type of learning style. They are really attentive to the smallest of details.

Logical students do well in traditional educational settings because those environments encourage them to take notes, do self-evaluations, and learn from their own mistakes. When taking part in a group activity or when confronted with anything that they believe defies logic, it drives them to frustration. They thrive when there is both structure and routine in their lives.

When students are learning a new language, they want to have scheduled courses and a clear curriculum so that they can track their progress and make the most of the time they spend studying.

Group Learners Versus Individual Learners

Group learners are individuals who prefer to learn in a group setting, where they can interact with their peers and receive feedback and support from others. This type of learning environment allows them to collaborate and share ideas, and they often feel more motivated and engaged when learning in a group.

Examples of group learning include study groups for a class or exam, team projects, discussions or debates, and collaborative problem-solving activities.

Individual learners, on the other hand, prefer to learn independently and at their own pace. They often prefer to work alone and can become easily distracted in group settings. They tend to be self-motivated and self-disciplined, and they often prefer to learn through reading, writing, and solitary problem-solving.

Examples of individual learning are self-study and independent research, solo projects or assignments, reading, and taking notes alone to reflect on later.

Students that have this type of learning style are most successful when they carry out activities such as research, homework, or exercises independently. They believe that when they work on a problem on their own, they are able to solve it more quickly and effectively.

Individualized instruction is beneficial for individuals learning a second language on their own, regardless of whether the instruction is delivered in-person, virtually, or through a combination of the two. One-on-one time with professors allows students to make more concentrated efforts in their advancement and increases the likelihood that they will be recognized for their unique achievements.

Learners that pursue their education on their own are self-driven, focused, and driven to succeed. Only when they are engaged in their academic pursuits are they likely to be solitary.

In contrast, some students learn best when they are among others. Being part of a group can sometimes motivate students to push themselves or try harder because they are thinking about what others in the group think about them. Other benefits of group learning are that it enhances communication and other professional development skills.

It's important to note that most people have a combination of both learning preferences, it's not only about being one type of learner but also, depending on the task and the subject, one may prefer a different learning style.

Chapter 5

Types of Language Processing

Children can develop language in different ways, two of which are as follows:

1. Analytical

2. Gestalt

Analytical Language Learners

Most neurotypicals analytically develop language. These children pay attention to and pick up on the meaning of individual words. After that, they may use that word in other circumstances before eventually fusing it with other words to create phrases and sentences. For example, a child may say milk when they see or want milk. They learn that the word for milk is used whether it comes from a jug, carton, cup, bottle, or from their mother's breast. They may begin to pair the word milk with another word after they have approximately fifty words in their repertoire.

For example, they may say "more milk" or "want milk." As they age and are exposed to more language, the average length of children's utterances will become longer. By age five or six, we would expect a sentence such as, "Mom, can I have milk, please?" Intonation use and understanding develop as a child gets older. Analytic language processors focus heavily on grammar from two to three years of age. As a result, their language is both flexible and productive. Most neurotypical children learn language this way.

Gestalt Language Learners

Gestalt language learners acquire language differently. They begin learning language by memorizing entire phrases rather than learning the meaning of one word at a time. The meaning of the words that make up those statements is then learned backward. Although some echolalia occurs naturally as a component of ordinary language development, many children often utilize both delayed and immediate echolalia. Echolalia used to be regarded as having no real meaning. Thus, statements like "You want some more?" were seen as the child repeating what they had heard before. But the recent researchers who promote neurodiversity are beginning to realize that is only sometimes the case.

Echolalia is sometimes referred to as scripting. Echolalia can look like the repetition of sounds, phrases, and movies from TV shows, humming, whistling, or singing. Other forms of echolalia may look like: copying any noise like a car or animal, as well as repeating words and phrases, including the tone in which it is produced. Echolalia can be defined as the literal and rote repetition of the speech of others. Echolalia presents as either immediate or delayed. Words repeated immediately or after a short time are referred to as immediate echolalia. This repetition can look like a single-word repetition at the end of a sentence, for example:

Adult: Are you hungry?

Child: Hungry.

It can also be a complete phrase repetition:

Adult: Let's get your shoes.

Child: Let's get your shoes.

Words that are heard by the child and are stored in their minds and then repeated after a long interval are referred to as delayed echolalia. Delayed echolalia can occur for a variety of reasons. Let's look at an example. A child may say: "line up at the door." He may be saying this phrase in his home because he wants to go somewhere, or he could be saying it because he is thinking about school, or he overheard you talking to someone about his teacher, and that phrase is something the teacher says every day.

Another example would be a family driving in a car, and as a particular song plays on the radio, it starts to rain. You, as the parent, say, "Oh no, would ya look at this." Two weeks later, the family is having a sunny Saturday afternoon barbeque while music plays in the background. The same song that was playing in the car sounds out of the radio at the barbecue, and your daughter says, "Oh no, would ya look at this." You can't work out why your daughter said those words. Now, every time she hears that song, she says, "Oh no! Would ya look at this!"... and you, as a parent, are confused as heck. The reason, however, is that she associated the statement with the song instead of the weather.

If the echolalia is an exact repetition, it is known as "pure." On the other hand, "mitigated" echolalia occurs when the child changes the original speaker's wording or intonation. As the child's understanding of language improves, an increase in mitigated echolalia may be observed.

Some children get great joy out of scripting familiar sounds or lines from their favorite people, movies, or songs. Some children use it to reassure themselves or to calm and cope with a stressful moment.

What Should You Do as a Parent if Your Child Communicates Via Echolalia?

There is nothing inherently wrong about being echolalic. As parents, we want our children to learn and grow and communicate with others. It is how we can share information and get our needs met. So, when toddlers or school-age children communicate with others, we want them to express themselves in a way that feels right and meets their needs. So, if the function of the echolalia is just to say something aloud because it has entertainment value, the speaker, if capable, might want to communicate that to the listener by saying something like, "I keep thinking about the movie *Star Wars*." It is especially crucial to convey this when the word, phrase, or sentence is off-topic or otherwise random to clarify why the phrase was said.

Remember that phrases spoken, or songs sung by a Gestalt Language Processor can have several different purposes. So, when a child is singing "itsy bitsy spider," they may think about a cute little spider climbing up a waterspout, or they may say it because they want to play with you. If and when we are not sure of the purpose of the echolalia, we must acknowledge that it is still communication and that we are listening but try to assign meaning to the utterance only if it is reasonably obvious.

Another example of delayed echolalia:

You are in the car line picking your child up from school. He gets into the car, and after you greet him, he says, "Are you thirsty"? What's happening here may need to be clarified initially because you think he is asking you a question. You may answer him by saying, "No, I'm not thirsty," only to realize he is asking you repeatedly. Your child memorized that statement as a whole, even though they might not have understood the meaning of each word. You then realize he doesn't want to know if you are thirsty; he has learned that when he hears that phrase, someone hands him a cup with a drink. He meant to communicate that he was thirsty. So, we now have to figure out how to give him the right words! The next time, before handing him the drink, you take his hand and gesture as if he is tapping his chest, and you model the words you want him to use, "I'm thirsty," and then hand him the drink. You have, then, just given him the words! Speaking from the child's frame of reference versus our own will help children who are echolalic know what to say. I always try to make sure I am making things as clear as possible for the child by making my comments or questions have a more dramatic tone, as well as prompting them somehow to indicate that we are referring to them.

If the child finds enjoyment through scripting favorite lines from movies at a time when you want their attention to be elsewhere, you can say something like, "I hear that you are thinking about the Toy Story movie. We are discussing what we will do after dinner tonight, so let's discuss that." By doing this, we are not abandoning the idea that the script may have some other meaning, as in the previous example about the doctor's office. Instead, we are trying to keep the topic of conversation clear.

Suppose the child is using scripting because they are anxious and need to self-regulate, calm, and provide self-reassurance; we would want to work toward finding additional calming and coping tools. Occupational therapy can be a wonderful resource. For example, the child may say, "Time to put your shoes on; it's OK," while having a major meltdown because they don't like how the shoes feel. We will not put them on the bus with bare feet, but we should still acknowledge their feelings about not wanting to wear the shoes. "I know you don't want to put your shoes on now, but it's time to go to school, and your feet are safe inside these shoes for now. I think we should look for a more comfortable pair this weekend, though."

It's essential to give him the most appropriate words from his frame of reference. For example, he is saying he doesn't want to wear the shoes, so we might want to model something like, "No shoes, please." When first learning the words, we want to honor the child's comments or requests, so they can connect what they say and the fact that it happens. For example, we would model or teach this when shoes are optional and then honor his request by allowing him to remain free of the shoes.

Rather than ask questions, it is better to model terms such as "Let's," "It's," and "I'm," so they are more likely to be communicating clearly. Intonation (the feeling behind the words) is another important tool that you can use to teach the words. So, when transitioning from the child's old phrase, "Are you thirsty?" to the phrase that reflects what they actually mean, "I'm thirsty," saying it with a strong emphasis on the "I'm" will make it more likely that the child will be able to remember and use it at the correct time. Keeping a record of your child's utterances can also be a helpful tool if you are willing to explore a little to figure out the meaning of the script based on how they are feeling at the moment. So, if your son says "Chika Chika Boom Boom" every time he is feeling ill, it may be because you read him that book the last time you were in the waiting room of the doctor's office. This scenario is an excellent example that echolalia is purposeful. He is communicating! We need to give him the words. "Let's go to the doctor" or "I'm sick" Delayed echolalia is often tied to things that are rich in emotions, so if you can pair the scripted phrase with a feeling or circumstance, you are more likely to discover the meaning of that phrase.

Hyperlexia

The term "hyperlexia" was first used in 1967. This characteristic is common in autism. Hyperlexic children are usually Gestalt Language Processors.

How we learn is influenced by how our brains process information. Children with autism frequently recognize the words but have trouble understanding the meaning of a sentence or paragraph. According to psychologist Robert Naseef, "This characteristic is common in autism. Children with autism often recognize the words but struggle to comprehend the meaning of the text or the paragraph" (Gordon, 2020). If a child can "read" before they are officially taught to read, they are likely hyperlexic. Once more, despite their ability to decipher the written language, young kids have trouble understanding what the paragraph is saying. So, they will see "ball" and be able to say "ball." When you or I see the word, and we say it (either in our heads or aloud), we are also picturing a ball in our minds. Hyperlexic children may or may not have that vision of the ball. Another example, they will see the words "Now it's time to go to the library," and they will say, "Now it's time to go to the library." These words do not necessarily conjure up thoughts of going to the library for the child. This difference between what they read and what they think is the comprehension piece that is often missing. So, when we think the child is reading, upon further evaluation, we realize they are indeed reading but not understanding. They also may need to learn the names of the individual letters or that words are symbols that represent real things. They may not know that we can combine letters to make words, combine words to make sentences, and combine sentences to make paragraphs. It's important to establish here that hyperlexia is not just an interest or obsession with lining up the letters of the alphabet in order from A to Z.

Regarding grammar, school-aged Gestalt language processors will not quickly understand how to put words together to say or write in more flexible ways.

We need to focus on the learning strengths of hyperlexic children and take into account the ways in which they are more likely to learn faster. Lists or instructions should be in bullet point form, with images next to the text. Explaining the "w" questions, such as "why," and then linking it to the start of the response "because" is a method that has proven effective. Interactive games and using a child's favorite points of interest, in addition to visual timetables, are also recommended.

Sign Language

While spoken language is certainly the more common means of communication, let's not forget about other forms of communication, such as sign language. I mentioned speech therapy in the echolalia section above, but it also applies to children that are completely non-verbal or that have difficulties speaking.

Adults and children are capable of expressing themselves visually through hand gestures, body language, facial expressions, and sign language.

Although sign language is the primary means of communication for the Deaf and Hard-of-Hearing community, it can also be helpful to other social groups. Sign language may be useful for communication for those with difficulties, including Autism, Apraxia of speech, Cerebral Palsy, and Down syndrome.

There is no universally recognized sign language. There are many variations of sign languages because, like spoken languages, they evolved naturally via interaction between various groups of people. Between 138 and 300 different sign languages are currently in use all over the world.

It's interesting to note that most nations with similar spoken languages do not necessarily have the same sign language. American Sign Language (ASL), British Sign Language (BSL), and Australian Sign Language are three variants of English, for instance (Auslan).

Recent years have seen an uptick in the popularity of introducing sign language to infants and toddlers. Some parents may be concerned that teaching their child sign language would impede their child's verbal development.

Research indicates that this is not the case. In fact, often, the use of signs paired with spoken words can lead to an increase in verbal abilities.

It's vital to differentiate between speech and language as a first step. Words are uttered using a sound process known as speech. It's the science of making sounds by manipulating the muscles in your mouth and airflow. The ability to communicate with others is facilitated by the use of language. Any combination of spoken words, physical actions, and graphic signs is possible.

Studies have revealed that exposing infants to sign language has no negative effects on their language development. The use of sign language has been shown to promote and stimulate linguistic growth. Simply put, it helps children get started with language sooner. Also, there are many benefits to learning a second language, both for verbal and nonverbal communication.

The five main benefits are:

1. Increased vocabulary.

2. Reduced temper tantrums due to boredom or dissatisfaction.

3. Growing capacity for social interaction.

4. Increased comprehension.

5. Increased production of more advanced linguistic skills

Early exposure to sign language has benefited a wide range of populations. Inclusion of children with expressive language difficulties, such as those caused by speech delays, Down syndrome, autism, and apraxia. Providing a method of communicating via sign is an additional way of communicating with your child with or without using spoken words.

In a nutshell, learning sign language can help a child's verbal and linguistic growth. Negative social behaviors are mitigated, positive ones are fostered, and mental frameworks are developed. When introduced at an early age, sign language aids in a child's emotional, social, and academic growth as well as linguistic development.

The use of a few simple hand signs not only assist newborns in communicating but also improve their parents' capacity to comprehend what it is that their babies are attempting to convey. Dialing down the frustration of not being able to communicate can help crank up their confidence that you will listen and respond.

Speech sounds develop during the early childhood years. Should there be no other mitigating factors, such as a difference in the oral cavity or dentition, we expect the latest developing speech sounds to develop between ages 5 and 8.

Is your toddler saying "dog"? Or is it "Dad"? And how can you distinguish whether they are attempting to tell you that they want more mashed sweet potatoes or that they want to get down from their high chair? It might be challenging to make sense of your baby's earliest attempts at communication, including their first words. This is especially true when the word is not accompanied by the item the child is referring to or if they are not using gestures.

Again, self-assurance is another benefit that can accrue to parents who study sign language, particularly first-time mothers and fathers. Learning baby signals cannot only help you and your baby communicate more effectively with one another, but it will also aid in the development of your baby's motor abilities. It may even increase their intelligence.

What Does Baby Sign Language Exactly Entail?

Baby sign language is frequently derived from American Sign Language (ASL), while some instructors may teach a variant of this language. The focus is on keywords that are important in your baby's world (think of "milk," "up," and "done") and is extremely fundamental. There is no introduction to advanced grammar or other body language complexities associated with full nonverbal communication.

When Should I Start Teaching My Neurodivergent Child Sign Language?

Beginning your child's sign language education between the ages of six and eight months is an excellent time to do it. Researchers, however, suggest that parents evaluate not just their baby's readiness but also their own, as signing needs learning on the part of the parent as well as a commitment to a significant amount of repetition of the relevant hand signs. Some parents are ready to start when their newborns are just a few months old, but others wait until their tiny ones are closer to a year old.

Which Signs Should I Begin With?

There are a few very helpful words, although any term that pertains to your baby's world has the potential to be helpful. Functional signs are an excellent place to begin. Examples of such indications are "milk" and "eat." but the fun ones are actually important as well because these are what your child will probably be most interested in practicing with you, and that is why the fun ones are actually important as well. These may include signs such as "dog" if your canine companion is already your infant's closest companion or "bath" if your child adores spending time in the bathtub.

Introduce between one to three signals at a time, being sure to reiterate them frequently as though you were making solid claims and signing the phrases while saying them out loud simultaneously. Researchers recommend avoiding using the signals as inquiries because doing so can cause your child to get confused. In other words, you are signing "milk" as a statement, not signing "milk" to ask if he wants it.

The top eight signs that are beneficial for neurodivergent babies to learn:

1. milk

2. more

3. all done

4. pick me up (done as a single sign)

5. help

6. mom/dad

7. give me

8. eat

Augmentative and Alternative Communication

With all the information sharing on social media, the understanding and use of augmentative and alternative forms of communication are on the rise. The term "augmentative and alternative communication" refers to any technology, systems, tactics, or tools for communication that either completely replaces or supplements natural speech (AAC). A person who has difficulty communicating through speech may benefit from the use of these technologies.

The first "A" in AAC stands for Augmentative Communication. When something is augmented, it is added to or supplemented in some way. The addition of anything to one's speech or lack of speech is an example of augmentative communication (e.g., sign language, pictures, a letter board). Your message might become more understandable to your audience as a result of this. If a child's speech is moderate to severely unintelligible, they may benefit from the use of AAC.

The term "alternative communication" is represented by the 2nd "A" in AAC. There can be several reasons why someone is or has become non-speaking; it may be temporary or permanent. Either way, an alternative way of communicating should be considered.

AAC can refer to tools, systems, equipment, or even methods in its most basic form. When a person is unable to rely on speech alone to communicate, these tools enable them to do so. It's possible that your child hasn't started talking yet. It's possible that you've lost your ability to communicate verbally. It's possible that your speech is inconsistent. If speaking is a challenging form of communication, AAC might be beneficial.

Who Does the AAC Serve?

There are a variety of circumstances that can prevent a person from effectively communicating through the use of voice. It's possible that they have a developmental issue that prevents them from developing speech properly. It's possible that a person had a brain injury that affects their ability to communicate verbally. AAC can be useful for a large number of people who struggle with a variety of communication issues, speech disorders, and speech impairments. Neurodivergent individuals benefit very much from AAC as well.

There are several different types of AAC, each with its own unique features and advantages.

Manual Communication Boards

These are communication boards that are held by the individual or their communication partner. They typically include a set of pictures or words that the individual can point to or use to express themselves.

Voice Output Devices

These devices speak for the individual, either through pre-recorded messages or by synthesizing speech. These devices can be portable and can vary from simple single message devices to more complex devices with multiple messages and capabilities like internet access.

Electronic Communication Devices

These devices are similar to Voice Output Devices. Still, they are more advanced and include a variety of features such as text-to-speech, email, and internet access.

Sign Language

Sign language is a visual form of communication that uses hand gestures, facial expressions, and body language to convey meaning. It is often used by individuals who are deaf or hard of hearing.

Speech Generating Devices

These devices enable the individual to produce speech by pressing a button or touching a screen. These devices can also include a variety of features, such as text-to-speech, email, and internet access.

Eye-gaze Systems

These systems allow individuals to communicate by using eye movements to select letters, words, or phrases from a computer screen.

It's imperative to understand that the most appropriate type of AAC will depend on the individual's specific needs and abilities. A speech-language pathologist or other professional can help determine the best AAC option for an individual.

Also, talk about how to find out what AAC is appropriate for your child's needs. Having a conversation without using words. It is challenging to communicate without using words. People who are unable to talk will be at a disadvantage in a world that is predominantly spoken. When messages cannot be conveyed clearly, it can be difficult and frustrating for everyone involved. This is frustrating for both the individual who is not speaking and the one with whom they are communicating.

People who are non-speakers frequently have a lot of thoughts that they want to convey to others. How do they communicate these ideas to others?

When a person is unable to communicate verbally, those around them frequently form opinions about their level of expertise, potential, and capacity to think and learn.

A person who is mute will quickly realize that there are certain things that are straightforward to communicate (e.g., reaching for the TV remote to suggest you want to change the channel). They also come to realize that there are some concepts that are difficult to convey (e.g., that the TV show reminds you of a family member who is gone).

What Different Kinds of AAC Are Utilized Most Frequently?

When a person is unable to speak, alternative and augmentative communication (AAC) refers to all of the tools and tactics that can be used to communicate with that person. Quite frequently, we separate them into two categories: aided and unaided AAC.

Unaided AAC (Augmentative and Alternative Communication) refers to communication methods that do not require external aids or devices. Examples of unaided AAC include sign language, facial expressions, and gestures, which rely solely on the person's body and language skills.

Assisted AAC (Augmentative and Alternative Communication) refers to communication methods that require external aids or devices to supplement or replace speech. Examples of assisted AAC can include communication boards, choice cards, and photo exchange systems, which can support individuals with communication impairments to express their needs, thoughts, and ideas.

- symbol boards

- cards with a choice

- books about methods of communication

- PODD books

- keyboards with a chart of the alphabet

- gadgets that generate speech or devices that facilitate communication

- AAC apps on mobile devices

For communication support, we might employ a high-tech gadget like a voice-generating device or an app on a tablet or phone. As an alternative, we could use a manual or low-tech tool. a journal or book for communication.

An example of a high-tech augmentative and alternative communication device is Proloquo on the iPad (Printed Proloquo board)

AAC That Is Text-based

An augmentative and alternative communication (AAC) system may be a text-based system with a keyboard. This is typically for a person who composes their thoughts on the computer before speaking. They typically have reading and spelling abilities. AssistiveWare's alternative augmentative communication (AAC) solution is called Proloquo4Text.

AAC Based on Symbols

When it comes to communication, a lot of people need drawings or symbols. This includes those individuals who are unable to read or spell at this time. Words or even phrases could be represented by graphical symbols that we could introduce. They can easily read people, including interpreting their body language, tone of voice, and emotions displayed on their faces.

If you want to access some more information on AAC, there is a non-profit organization that focuses on education called MCIE. They are not specifically autism education structured, but there is a very interesting article on their blog, accompanied by videos made either by non-speaking autistic individuals or videos about AAC. Follow the link below:

www.thinkinclusive.us/post/videos-films-augmentative-alternative-communication

Chapter 6

Words at School

The Individuals with Disabilities Education Act (IDEA) is a federal law that mandates special education services to children with disabilities. The law has two primary components: Part B and Part C. Part B mandates special education services for children aged three to twenty-one. At the same time, Part C provides early intervention services to infants and toddlers aged zero to three.

Part C: Early Intervention Services

Part C of IDEA is designed to provide early intervention services to infants and toddlers with developmental delays or disabilities. Early intervention services are provided to children and their families from birth through age two. These services are designed to identify, evaluate, and provide early intervention services to children with disabilities to support their development and ensure they are ready for school when the time comes.

An Individualized Family Service Plan (IFSP) is a document developed for children with disabilities who are receiving early intervention services under Part C of IDEA. The IFSP outlines the child's strengths and needs, as well as the goals and objectives of the early intervention services. It also includes information about the family's priorities, resources, and child development concerns.

To obtain an IFSP, parents must first request an evaluation from their local early intervention agency or state lead agency. The evaluation must be conducted within 45 days of the request. Once the evaluation is complete, the early intervention team, including the family, will meet to develop the IFSP. The team will include professionals from various disciplines, such as early childhood educators, therapists, medical professionals, and the child's family. The team will review assessment results, identify the child's strengths and needs, and develop measurable goals and objectives. The IFSP must be reviewed every six months and updated annually to ensure that the child's progress is monitored and that the services provided are appropriate for their needs.

Child Find: Part B

Child Find is a component of Part B of IDEA, which requires schools to identify and evaluate children with disabilities. The goal of Child Find is to locate and evaluate all children with disabilities, regardless of the severity of their condition. Child Find applies to children ages three to twenty-one, including children in private schools or the homeless.

Qualifying Conditions for IEP

To qualify for an Individualized Education Plan (IEP), a child must have one or more of the thirteen qualifying conditions listed under IDEA. These conditions include Autism, Deaf-Blindness, Deafness, Emotional Disturbance, Hearing Impairment, Intellectual Disability, Multiple Disabilities, Orthopedic Impairment, Other Health Impairments, Specific Learning Disability, Speech or Language Impairment, Traumatic Brain Injury, and Visual Impairment.

Getting an Evaluation: Starting the Process

Parents who suspect that their child may have a disability that requires special education services can initiate the evaluation process by contacting their child's school or local education agency (LEA). Once a request is made for an evaluation, the school must respond promptly and provide the parent with a copy of the procedural safeguards notice, which explains the parents' rights under IDEA.

Goals of Part C and Part B

The primary goal of Part C is to provide early intervention services to infants and toddlers with disabilities to support their development and ensure that they are ready for school when the time comes. The primary goal of Part B is to provide children with disabilities with free and appropriate public education (FAPE) in the least restrictive environment (LRE) possible. The LRE means that children with disabilities should be educated with their peers without disabilities to the maximum extent appropriate.

Procedural Safeguards

IDEA provides parents with procedural safeguards to ensure that they are involved in the decision-making process and that their child's rights are protected. Some of the procedural safeguards provided by IDEA include the right to obtain an independent evaluation, the right to participate in the development of their child's IEP, the right to access their child's educational records and the right to due process.

Federal vs. State Law Concerning IDEA

Under IDEA, each state is required to develop policies and procedures for providing special education services to children with disabilities. States must comply with the requirements of IDEA, but they also have the flexibility to implement their policies and procedures. State laws cannot conflict with IDEA but can provide additional protections and services for children with disabilities.

Although each state is required to comply with the requirements of IDEA, there may be some differences in how the law is implemented from state to state. Here are three examples of how the laws of IDEA may differ from state to state:

1. Eligibility Criteria: While the thirteen qualifying conditions for receiving an IEP are set by federal law, states may have additional criteria for eligibility. For example, some states may require that a child's disability must have an adverse effect on their academic performance before they are eligible for an IEP, while other states may not have this requirement.

2. Timelines: IDEA sets specific timelines for various aspects of the special education process, such as the timeline for completing an evaluation or developing an IEP. However, states may have specific timelines that differ from federal timelines. For example, some states may require that an IEP meeting be held within a shorter timeframe than the federal requirement.

3. Procedural Safeguards: IDEA provides parents with procedural safeguards to protect their rights and ensure they are involved in decision-making. While federal law outlines these safeguards, states may have their own additional procedural safeguards. For example, some states may require that parents be provided with an interpreter or translator during the special

education process if they do not speak English.

Chapter 7

Words at Home

Everyone should make an effort to gain an understanding of the notion of neurodiversity and incorporate it into their perspective of the world. Throughout human history, society has traditionally put the responsibility for socialization, communication, and "typical" behavior on individuals who are autistic or neurodiverse.

The concept of neurodiversity enables us to comprehend the many modes of relating to other people, talking with them, and existing in the world as merely the natural and typical variations that are inherent to the human experience. When we follow the tenets of neurodiversity, we cease trying to transform autistic and neurodivergent people to become more "normal" (or neurotypical). Instead, we seek to establish understanding across all different sorts of neurotypes. When viewed through this lens, validating and accepting individual ways of becoming the responsibility of each and every person.

There is no other setting that has a greater influence on the experiences that a child has while growing up than their own home. Therefore, during the course of this chapter, we are going to talk about neurodiversity at home and what will help make your house more accepting of neurodiversity.

What can we do to make our homes more comfortable for neurodivergent children and adolescents? Here are a couple of things:

Provide a Secure Environment in Which Your Child Can Feel Comfortable Being Themselves

It is important for children to have the sense that they can be themselves when they are at home. There is a lot of demand in the outside world to comply with various forms of communication, thinking, and being. This pressure can make it difficult to be oneself. For neurodivergent adolescents, this can lead to masking or taking on behaviors that aren't true to who they are for the advantage of making others happy or comfortable.

In order to include activities that are accepting of neurodiversity in your household, encourage your children to investigate the various aspects of themselves that they might normally feel pressured to keep hidden from the rest of the world. Validate that it is okay for your autistic or neurodiverse child to stim freely in the comfort of their own home.

Become Aware of Your Child's Requirements and Meet Them

Needs extend well beyond those that are often addressed in a class context as the fundamental requirements for surviving. Our requirements may be broken down into three categories: our physiological needs, which include things like the requirement for food, water, and shelter; our sensory needs; and our activity and interest needs. There is a good chance that your sensory needs, as well as the needs for activity and interest, will not be the same as those of your child.

Everyone, regardless of their neurotype, has a unique experience of the stimulus that their senses provide. This can include elements like lights, sounds, or even how clothing feels on the body. Getting to know what feels comfortable for your child's senses will allow you to change the environment to match their requirements.

Individuals have varying requirements in terms of their ideal activities and interests. A good life balance for many neurotypical people requires spending a significant amount of time in the company of other people. Alternately, the activity and interest needs of certain neurotypical individuals, as well as many neurodivergent individuals, revolve primarily around more solo pursuits.

Recognize That the Needs of Your Child May Differ From the Expectations that You Have of Them

If your child's neurotype is different from yours, it is essential to acknowledge the possibility that their requirements and your expectations will not align perfectly. The majority of individuals are made aware of the concept that there is a "typical" set of needs and that the things that many other people describe as needs are actually desires rather than necessities. It is essential to dispute this notion inside yourself (for example, why wouldn't we consider the needs of all people as valid?) and to make your child aware of the fact that various people have varied requirements in their lives.

If your child is neurotypical, this may look like helping them recognize that no, they do not get to have a fidget toy in class even though their neurodivergent peer does because their neurodivergent peer requires that fidget toy to be able to listen to the teacher's lesson, while they do not.

If you have a child who is neurodivergent, this may involve assisting them in understanding that it is acceptable to require the use of a fidget toy while in school, even while their peers do not. That is a need that they have, and it is important to remember that all needs are legitimate.

Let Your Child Communicate in the Methods That Are Most Comfortable for Them

Certain modes of communication, without a shadow of a doubt, receive the highest marks from society. The term "types" refers to both the mode of communication (such as expressive voice, gesture, American Sign Language, Alternative, and Augmentative Communication, etc.) as well as the style of communication (e.g., direct, indirect, tangential, etc.).

A child's unique form of communication and manner of expression can be validated in a straightforward manner by recognizing that the mode of expression they employ is not only entirely appropriate and valid but also does not require any sort of correction.

How many times have you encouraged your child to "use their words" if they speak a language that was traditionally spoken in your home? Why? Why is it necessary for your child to use words to communicate if they can show you what they want by reaching for something or pushing something away while it's in front of them? Their way of communicating is efficient and unambiguous!

Your ability to help your child in a way that affirms their neurodiversity will be enhanced if you allow your child the freedom to communicate in the ways that are most comfortable, natural, and efficient for them.

Foster Better Communication and Mutual Understanding Among Family Members

The first step in developing a home environment that is accepting of neurodiversity is being familiar with both yourself and your child. When you are able to notice the parallels as well as the differences in the needs and ways of being among the members of your family, you will be in a better position to address those differences with openness and curiosity.

Acceptance comes as a gift to us when we finally let go of the idea that neurotypical people are in the right and those with neurodivergent traits are in the wrong. We will stop fighting to change our children from who they are and instead focus on learning to understand them and assisting them in understanding that there are other ways of talking, socializing, and living that are equal.

Being a sibling of an autistic child is not the same as being a parent, and it has its own unique challenges. I am going to include a link to a video on an Australian parenting website, where siblings of children on the spectrum talk about their experiences and relationships. It features an 18-year-old university student called Eryl, who has a sister named Ellis, with Aspergers, and a 10-year-old called Bryce, who has two autistic siblings. It is very interesting and definitely worth a watch.

raisingchildren.net.au/autism/children-autism-videos/siblings-of-autistic-children

Challenges That Parents of Neurodivergent Children May Face

"Autism is part of my child, it's not everything he is. My child is so much more than a diagnosis" (Coehlo, n.d.).

Many parents who have children with autism are true superheroes. They provide a foundation of support and open doors for people who are exceptionally talented and have unique qualities. Every day presents the family with fresh obstacles to overcome as well as new chances. I have compiled a list of some of the most common difficulties that parents of children with ASD face on a daily or weekly basis in this part of the book.

The following is a list of common challenges that come with parenting a neurodivergent child:

Finances

When it comes to the cost of raising a child on the autism spectrum, some parents may feel overwhelmed by the long-term financial commitment. This might be the situation in households that do not have access to medical insurance, for example. The financial burden can manifest itself in a variety of ways, including the use of one's own vehicle rather than public transportation, the hiring of a carer on a regular basis, the giving up of a job in order to take care of the child, and the rising costs that are associated with the raising of a child. Having said that, we all have financial burdens to bear, and if we are smart as parents of autistic children, we can give our children what they need to function optimally without breaking the bank. Don't forget, as per the section on education in the previous chapter, the Individuals with Disabilities Education Act (IDEA) facilitates free public education to eligible children with disabilities throughout the United States. Some good planning and knowledge can save you money in a way that does not prejudice your child.

Stress and Lack of Time for Self-Care

It is not an easy undertaking to provide care for children who are autistic. It is not without its share of difficulties, strain, and ups and downs along the way. Because every child is different, providing care for children who have autism spectrum disorder (ASD) or any other neurodivergent disorder could be a full-time job for some families and parents. Every child has their own unique set of challenges, varying degrees of severity, and so on. Taking care of children is a source of stress for all types of families, particularly for single parents and nuclear families. Their already high levels of stress are made much worse by the fact that they may not have the support and aid of other family members or extended family members, etc.

When a parent or both parents do not have the assistance of a paid carer, extended family, or even close family members, they may find it difficult to provide enough care for their child, maintain good performance at one or more jobs, take care of the household, and multitask well. Because of this, they have very little time, if any, to spend on themselves. This could entail little to no opportunity for social interaction, rest, physical activity, the pursuit of hobbies and interests, and so on. The care of the child or adolescent with all of their particular intricacies can take precedence over the person's own identity, which could be pushed into the background. There are ways to take little breaks from life, so to speak, during which time you can display kindness towards yourself. Everyone will tell you that exercise is a great form of escapism. Think about it, if you're cranking the treadmill up to full speed, you definitely do not have the ability to stress and overthink. The additional positive element is dopamine production from physical activity. Maybe you enjoy swimming, walking or reading. Whatever it is, take some time out for yourself and don't restrict yourself to the identity of "the parent of the autistic child."

Mindfulness

Cognitive Behavioral Therapy (CBT), which includes mindfulness, is a set of exercises that can be practiced on one's own or facilitated by a therapist.

It is a way of being kind to yourself and includes a deep focus on what may seem to be mundane. Don't rush things but rather observe the trees and flowers, their intricacies, and their beauty. When you sip your coffee, enjoy the sensory experience and focus only on that moment. The idea is to distract yourself from the stress of life in general by being present and giving your attention to what you are doing at that particular time. You can find guided mindfulness meditation on YouTube, Spotify, Apple Music, and many other platforms. These guided meditations involve relaxing music and a calming voice guiding you through close observation of your breathing, your wiggling toes, and other body sensations. I am not going to go into more detail, but I encourage readers to explore this avenue as a "me time" opportunity.

Challenges in Terms of Communication

Some youngsters who are neurodivergent have difficulty with verbal communication. Communication is a challenge for the parents of these children, which adds to the stress and anxiety that the parents already feel. The inability of their child to convey their requirements and preferences presents a barrier for the parents. The tribulations of parenting are made more difficult by the fact that youngsters do tend to struggle to read nonverbal communication and cues. As parents, we are aware of this, and being aware, in turn, empowers us to work on these difficulties with our children. Just a reminder that our autistic children are different. There is nothing "wrong" or "broken."

Stigmatization

There are many people on this planet, and therefore there are numerous responses to various scenarios and individuals. There are certain people who are not sensitive, compassionate, or accepting. The adverse reactions have a direct and personal influence on the child as well as on the parents, and unfortunately, the repercussions can last for some time. Breaking the stigma or at least making a dent in it can be done by raising awareness and getting people to start having conversations about autism. The three YouTube channels that I referred to earlier are doing just that, but it can be done on a much smaller scale. A short presentation at your child's school or an informative article in a local newspaper, in addition to encouraging friends and family to do their own research, all help.

How can parents efficiently face these challenges at home and enable their children to be comfortable? What better way to try to navigate these challenges than to take advice from and listen to the struggles of parents who have faced the same things?

raisingchildren.net.au created a video talking about the various experiences of parents with children on the spectrum. Here are the comments from some of the parents in their own words.

Alison (mother of two children, including one Autistic child)

When you're battling with something you don't really understand, there's a huge learning curve, so a lot of the initial time is spent just trying to understand what's going on. Because I've got two children, we've got two children. You don't parent them the same. The way we parent our neurotypical daughter is very, very different from the way we parent Ellis. That was a huge learning curve because you can't parent them the same way. It doesn't work. And that's hard. Umm, people again cannot understand why it looks like you're letting him get away with things when you're really not.

Bobby (father of two children, including one autistic child)

There are a lot of challenges, challenges with his development, and challenges with his speech. How would he go to primary school? Would he be set back in certain situations? For example, if he gets bullied, would he be set back? And then all the work we've done won't be a waste but will be very disappointing because of something that's happening outside of our control. Our biggest challenges are just basically helping Peter become a little boy—a five-year-old little boy—that's like every other five-year-old little boy, who wants to just go out there and play and be accepted for who he is, not what he has.

Jane (mother of two children, including one Autistic child)

I think one of the hardest things is the fact that he doesn't enjoy people's company. I mean, we are social creatures, so it's really hard to see a child just want to be by themselves all the time.

Sharon (mother of two children, including one autistic child)

There was probably a period when Peter—the communication wasn't coming—and that was a really, really difficult period, so between two-and-a-half and three-and-a-half was probably the most turbulent year we'd had. Umm, because we didn't know what he wanted, how he wanted it when he wanted it. And that's where the PECs—the picture exchange cards – really helped and encouraged him to sort of make that initiation and that communication when it was something that he really wanted.

Shannon (father of four children, including three autistic children)

I'd like to be able to understand what Dominic's thinking when he's doing his really intense arm flaps—that's what the hardest thing is: We don't know why. He can be sitting here happy as anything, playing with his car, and the next thing his arms are going, and he's getting really intense. Before, it was just sort of his arms flapping [moves hands to demonstrate], but now he sort of twists his hand around and sort of moves his body [demonstrates with arm], and he goes really rigid. But when he's really involved in it, you can't get him out. You can see him try to break out of it, which is hard to see.

Marita (mother of two autistic children)

I think the most challenging thing is actually just all the little things you have to keep on top of. So, you have to remember what you're saying. Heidi, because of her sensory needs, she won't eat food that touches, so when I make macaroni and cheese for dinner, there's a bowl of macaroni, there's the cheese sauce, and then there are the vegetables. And she dips them into the cheese sauce, and it's all separate. And I have to remember these things, and if I accidentally make them together, it's a disaster. And having to remember the right toy to go to bed with or, you know, it's Tuesday. I need this special thing for school because it's Tuesday. The little things, they kind of buildup, and at the end of the week, I fall to pieces because I'm exhausted trying to remember it all through the week.

Joanne (mother of four children, including two autistic children)

The challenges I found, umm, even now, though my children are in school, the constant challenge is they're always behind. They`re always behind academically, so you're always playing catch-up, so it's that constant "OK, what can I do next? How can I teach her to tell the time? How can I try and get her to tie her shoelaces?" And it's that you're always pushing. It keeps you awake at night; it keeps you awake at night as to "OK, what can I do now to help my child?"

Rachel (mother of four children, including three autistic children)

The biggest challenge, like for my personal challenge, is learning to pick and choose what is really relevant. So, I want to pick my battles and not sweat the small stuff, and spend my energy on the big stuff.

Joanne

There are extra financial burdens with special needs children. There's the fact that you ignore your husband more because you're spending so much time focusing on the children and their learning abilities. So, it's a lot more... harder on a marriage, yes. But we've hung in there [laughs].

Sharon

I guess it's really important that you make time as a couple. But sometimes it's not always possible. I mean, we're very lucky that my father-in-law and my mother-in-law are a great support network. Peter has sleepovers there all the time, so we get a respite in that respect. That's not a luxury that a lot of people have in our position. And, umm, but it's really important that we can just switch off because I think just as much as there is a risk of Peter being, if you like, over-therapized, and having everyday sort of, "What therapy do we need to be doing today?" Umm, I think he needs to have that level of non-structure, just as much as we need a relief or a break from the structured events in the day sometimes, just to let loose and do what we like.

Peter (father of two children, including one with Asperger's)

Get as much help as you can. Don't be afraid to ask. There's a lot of support out there, but you have to go and look for it. And you really have to, umm, where we were ten years ago—well, I suppose six, seven, eight years ago—I don't think there was that awareness that there is now. And it's much more prominent than it was. The avenues have opened up a little bit to access help, but you really still have to knock down doors, find individuals who will support you, and hang onto them, but just use every avenue that you've got to get help.

Marita

There are struggles; it's not always easy. But it's not always really hard, either. There are times when I just go, "That's amazing." We're walking down the street during Autumn, and the leaves are being blown out of the trees, and Heidi goes, "The leaves are pouring down." Because it looks like they're just being poured down, and that amazing way of seeing things so differently—I just love it.

Emotional Support for Parents

An important thing to recognize is that even superheroes sometimes require assistance, and there is absolutely no shame in that. To be able to provide a comfortable home environment for neurodivergent children, parents first need to make sure that their own mental health is in check, and research has shown time and again that parents who seek therapy often do better with their children.

In a recent study, a group of researchers came to the conclusion that parents who engage in cognitive therapy with their children who have autism also enjoy improvements in their own ability to regulate their moods and emotions. It is estimated that over 70percent of children with autism struggle with emotional or behavioral issues. These children may benefit from cognitive behavior therapy to enhance their capacity to control their emotions and improve their overall functioning.

The researchers came to the conclusion that parents who take part in cognitive treatment with their children also enjoy a genuine advantage that contributes to an enhanced quality of life for the entire family. "When parents bring their children in for cognitive behavior therapy, the vast majority of the time, they are shown to a separate room where they are educated on what their children are doing, and they are not considered to be co-therapists. What we found to be particularly interesting about our research is the dynamic that emerges when parents are actively involved in all stages of the process. We are now able to demonstrate that it is beneficial for the parents of children diagnosed with autism, in addition to the fact that it is beneficial for the children themselves." said Jonathan Weiss, Ph.D., a CIHR Chair in Autism Spectrum Disorders

(ASD) Treatment and Care Research. in addition to being an Associate Professor in the Department of Psychology in the Faculty of Health (Weiss, 2017).

Therapy is beneficial for autistic children, but it also has a significant positive impact on the parents. In a recent study, a group of researchers came to the conclusion that parents who engage in cognitive therapy with their children who have autism also enjoy improvements in their own ability to regulate their moods and emotions. It is estimated that over 70percent of autistic children struggle with emotional or behavioral issues. These children may benefit from cognitive behavior therapy to enhance their capacity to control their emotions and improve their overall functioning.

The parents who participated in the study were given the opportunity to take part in a controlled random experiment. They were asked to fill out surveys both before and after the treatment, and their responses were compared to those of parents who had not yet started therapy. During the course of a trial of cognitive behavior therapy for children with autism spectrum disorder (ASD) aged 8 to 12 who did not have an intellectual disability, Weiss and Ph.D. student Andrea Maughan investigated how parents' mental health, mindfulness, and perceptions of their children changed over the course of the study.

For the purposes of the study, parents were given the role of co-therapists with the professional who was treating their children, and they were tasked with implementing the same tactics alongside their children. Because of this, the parents were able to learn how to assist themselves throughout the procedure. During the activities, parents were obligated to keep a journal of their children's ideas and reactions. "As a parent who took part in the SAS: OR Program, I experienced the same level of personal development as my child did. With my son, I used to employ a strategy of "one size fits all;" now, both he and I have various tools at our disposal to help us navigate through challenging situations. Our lives have been enriched with positivity and comfort as a result of our ability to communicate our feelings, recognize triggers, and think proactively about potential ways. According to Jessica Jannarone, a mother who participated in the research project, the most meaningful part of her involvement was "seeing my child mature in this program and finding a method to start handling his feelings."

According to the findings of the study, when parents participated in cognitive therapy with their children, they saw changes in their own levels of sadness, as well as in their ability to regulate their emotions and be more mindful parents. It helped them become more aware of their parenting and all of the good they do as parents, which is something that helped them become more aware of their parenting and all of the good they do as parents. The research showed that parents improved their abilities to handle their own emotions and to see themselves in a more positive light.

The findings of this study also highlight how important it is for healthcare practitioners to involve the child's parents in the process of providing care to the child when the child has autism. Weiss summed up his findings by stating in the conclusion that "we know that parents of children with autism endure substantial levels of distress in addition to all of the wonderful experiences they have." Therefore, if there is anything that can be done to lessen that, we have an obligation to make an effort to do so. The findings of the study were presented in an article that was published in the Journal of Autism and Developmental Disorders.

This study, and many more, continue to shed light on exactly how important it is for parents to seek therapy alongside their children. You know what they say on all of our flights, put your own oxygen mask on before helping others.

Chapter 8

Growing Pains

Researchers are just starting to understand what goes on in the brains of Neurodivergent children during the adolescent years to explain the distinct social, cognitive, and emotional issues that these individuals face.

For Neurodivergent children and adolescents, puberty can be a very trying time. As neurodivergent people age sexually and become more eager in friendships and relationships, it can be difficult for them to cope with the symptoms of autism, which include difficulties with sensory and emotional processing, actions that are repetitive, and a lack of social nuance. As a result of their inability to comprehend the complexities of the relationships between neurotypical girls, neurodivergent girls may have an especially difficult time interacting socially. One study conducted in 2006 found that 72 percent of 109 autistic children experienced depression, anxiety, or another mental health issue. Eating disorders are also uncommonly widespread in autistic adolescents. Comparatively, a survey conducted in 2016 on more than 50,000 neurotypical children and adolescents found that fewer than 20% of them suffer from a mental health disorder (Magnuson, 2016).

In the meantime, the process of quicker long-distance signaling in the brain occurs during adolescence. This occurs as bundles of nerve fibers grow coated in fatty insulation, thus forming new neural highways. This remodeling of the brain usually results in increased cognitive abilities, such as improved problem-solving, as well as emotional maturity and a heightened sense of identity. And despite the fact that many young people on the spectrum exhibit comparable improvement, there is a sizable population that does not.

Although puberty has been compared to a roller coaster, it is a slow and bumpy ride. It manifests itself in stages and entails profound alterations to the structure and function of the brain. During this period of time, the brain eliminates any neural connections (synapses) that were created during the first ten to fifteen years of life but were never utilized. Before adolescence, the areas of the brain that are responsible for basic sensory and motor processes begin to undergo pruning. The dorsolateral prefrontal cortex, which is involved in higher cognitive tasks such as impulse control, decision-making, judgment, social skills, and emotional regulation, is one of the areas that are among the last to undergo this maturation process.

Growing up autistic or neurodivergent can be a challenging but ultimately rewarding experience for the individual. Autistic adolescents with ASD may have difficulties forming relationships, which is one of the challenges they confront. Because it can be challenging to interpret nonverbal clues such as body language, it can be challenging to take part in conversations or to build friendships with other people.

On the other hand, many autistic adolescents are exceptionally knowledgeable and provide fresh points of view on the world. They may be exceptionally gifted in the areas of music or art, or they may excel in academics.

Neurodiverse adolescents and their families may face a number of challenges as they navigate the complexities of growing up. Finding a method of communication that is both efficient and successful is one of the most difficult difficulties. Because many neurodiverse adolescents are nonspeaking, it can be challenging for them to communicate their requirements and preferences. Frustration and other behavioral problems may result from this. In addition, having trouble communicating might make it difficult to interact with other people and form connections with them.

However, there are many things that one can do to smooth out the transition period from childhood to adolescence.

- Build a solid foundation: Start early and build a strong foundation of communication skills, including nonverbal communication strategies such as gestures, pictures, or communication devices.

- Develop coping skills: Adolescence can be a time of heightened stress, so it's important to develop coping skills for you and your child. For example, practice relaxation techniques and identify trusted individuals who can provide support.

- Encourage self-expression: Help your child find ways to express themselves, such as through art, music, or writing. This can also help develop communication skills.

- Foster independence: Encourage your child's independence by gradually increasing their responsibilities and practicing hygiene, dressing, and meal preparation skills.

- Develop a transition plan: Develop a transition plan that outlines the goals and objectives for your child during adolescence. This can include educational, vocational, and independent living goals.

- Stay connected: Connect with your child's healthcare providers, educators, and community resources. Seek support from other parents going through similar experiences, and consider joining a support group.

Foster Independence

Your adolescent with neurodivergence will benefit much from your assistance in cultivating autonomous abilities that will serve them well as they enter adulthood. This could entail things like cooking, cleaning, making a budget, and figuring out how to get around using public transit.

A Neurodiversity-affirming Approach to Social Skills

As we know, neurodiversity is the idea that autistic individuals have differences and not deficits. Ableist language refers to the language used when referring to a disability as something negative. We know that being autistic is not being disabled, but words or phrases like "dumb," "I'm OCD," and "special needs" are offensive and can lead to those awful feelings of isolation. Basically, we need to focus on differences and the positive side of those differences.

We don't want to teach neurodiverse children to imitate neurotypical social skills. This can cause the neurodiverse child to learn to "mask." Masking is harmful to the ND person. For example, typical social skills training goals often attempt to minimize the appearance of autistic characteristics to get someone to blend in, which is harmful to self-esteem and identity.

Start Preparing for Adjustments

The teenage years are, at times, marked by both significant and subtle life shifts. Discussing these upcoming shifts in advance can be of great assistance to your autistic adolescent's preparation for them. It's possible that this will help you feel more in control of your life and less anxious. Encourage them to take part in the planning process and present them with options that will empower them whenever you can.

Encourage Good Self-Esteem

It is critical for a neurodivergent to have a positive self-image and sense of accomplishment. Praise your adolescent child's abilities and acknowledge their achievements to encourage the development of a healthy, positive self-image in them. Take pictures of meaningful events so that you can celebrate accomplishments and commemorate reaching personal milestones in a way that your child may enjoy.

How to Deal with the Adolescent Period When Your Child is Neurodivergent

The adolescent years can be difficult for anybody, but for people with neurodivergence, the move into puberty can have a significant and devastating influence on their lives. Autistic teenagers frequently have to contend with increased anxiety and heightened sensitivity to sensory input. This is in addition to the normal physical and hormonal changes that all teenagers go through. As a consequence of this, they could have difficulties at school, in their communities, and in communicating with other people.

There are, nevertheless, steps that can be taken to make the transition into neurodivergent adolescence less challenging. One method is therapy, which focuses on providing patients with positive reinforcement and instructing them in new skills in manageable increments. Finding an experienced therapist who is also autistic and understands the condition is essential. Teenagers who have autism are capable of overcoming the particular difficulties that come with being on the spectrum if they have the appropriate support system in place.

In addition, parents and other carers can lend support and understanding while also assisting in the establishment of reasonable boundaries and objectives for their children. Parents and other carers can assist in making the transition into adulthood easier for neurodiverse individuals and their families if they take the appropriate supportive actions throughout this time of life.

Giving Teenagers the Words

Self-advocacy is the ability to speak up for oneself and communicate one's needs and desires. It's an essential skill for all teenagers, but particularly important for autistic teenagers with unique needs and challenges.

Self-advocacy can help autistic teenagers take ownership of their lives and advocate for accommodations and support they need to succeed. It can also help them build confidence, improve self-esteem, and develop essential life skills.

However, many autistic teenagers may struggle with self-advocacy due to communication challenges. They may not know how to express their needs or feel uncomfortable speaking up for themselves.

Helping Autistic Teenagers Find Their Voice

There are several strategies that parents, teachers, and caregivers can use to help autistic teenagers find their voice and develop self-advocacy skills:

Encourage Communication: It's essential to create a supportive environment where autistic teenagers feel comfortable expressing themselves. Encourage communication in all forms, including verbal, written, and nonverbal. Our ability to handle comfort and confidence is made MUCH more straightforward when we encourage them to communicate about things they love and care about. Think about it this way, if you lived in a world where people wanted to share about something that didn't interest you all the time, you might want to communicate less. But if you had a few good friends who you shared interests with, you would be MUCH more likely to share your thoughts and feelings with them.

Practice Social Communication Skills: Social communication skills can be practiced and developed. Encourage autistic teenagers to practice initiating conversations, taking turns, and reading nonverbal cues with people they are comfortable with-not strangers.

Use Visual Supports: Visual supports such as pictures, symbols, and social stories can be helpful for autistic teenagers who struggle with communication. They can provide a visual cue for communication and help understand social situations.

Teach Self-Advocacy Skills: Autistic teenagers can learn self-advocacy skills through modeling and practice. Encourage them to speak up (it doesn't have to be verbal; they can send an email.) for themselves and provide opportunities to practice these skills in real-life situations.

Advocate for Accommodations: Parents, teachers, and caregivers can help autistic teenagers advocate for extra time on tests, preferential seating, and sensory support. These accommodations can help level the playing field and make it easier for autistic teenagers to communicate and learn.

Remember, their lives will likely change toward the end of their teen years as high school will end, and they may get a job, go to college, or start their own business. Prepare them as best as possible by teaching them what the world expects of them. Let them then decide how to proceed and when to communicate with others.

Learning in Tragedy

The stories above conjure different emotions and illustrate parental emotions too. As parents, we are always learning, but we need the assistance of teachers and therapists because at home, sometimes "normal" is not enough. Recently I came to identify something I already knew, but on a bigger level, while watching a Netflix documentary called *American Tragedy*. The parent of one of the Columbine shooters, Sue Klebold, was interviewed. It was surprising to learn how "normal" her son Dylan Klebold's life was before the shooting. He went to prom, his parents were married, and he had a rich life that involved hobbies and celebrations. As I watched and listened with an open mind, I wholeheartedly believed his mother when she spoke about the genuine shock of learning from the shooting. The disbelief and horror in her eyes and heart were palpable. When she talked about her relationship with her son, she said something to the effect of, this wasn't a child that was ignored or neglected; I was that mom who grabbed his face and looked him in the eyes and told him he was loved and that I was proud of him, on a more regular basis than most parents do! Mrs. Klebold understands teenagers more now than she did then. She acknowledges that there were conversations that they didn't have about thoughts and feelings. The documentary's takeaway was that the most effective approaches for social and emotional learning should be integrated into school curriculums and provide skill building across all grade levels to reach all children. The best social and emotional learning efforts are proactive, not reactive. That means we don't wait for problems to come up to deal with them. Instead, we prevent problems through our word choice. As a society, we want to ensure children cannot only recognize emotions and feelings but also give words to them.

Communication With an Autistic Partner

Be Clear and Direct: When communicating with an autistic partner, it's essential to be clear and direct. Avoid using figurative language, sarcasm, or indirect communication. Instead, use clear, concise language and express your needs and expectations.

Use Visual Supports: Visual supports such as pictures, diagrams, and written instructions can be helpful for autistic individuals who struggle with verbal communication. Use visual supports to supplement oral communication and provide additional cues for understanding.

Avoid Overstimulation: Autistic individuals may be sensitive to sensory input such as bright lights, loud noises, and certain textures. Avoid overstimulation during communication by creating a calm, quiet environment and minimizing distractions.

Practice Active Listening: Active listening involves paying attention to the speaker and providing feedback to show that you understand what they are saying. Practice active listening by repeating back what your partner has said, clarifying any misunderstandings, and asking questions for clarification.

Respect Differences: Autistic individuals may have different communication styles and preferences than neurotypical individuals. Respect these differences by acknowledging and valuing their unique perspective.

Create a Communication Plan: Creating a communication plan with your autistic partner can help establish clear expectations and boundaries around communication. This plan can include preferred modes of communication, strategies for managing misunderstandings, and guidelines for avoiding overstimulation.

Communication is essential to any successful relationship, but it can be particularly challenging when one or both partners are autistic. By understanding communication challenges and using clear and direct communication, visual supports, active listening, and respect for differences, we can improve communication in a relationship with an autistic person. It's important to remember that communication is a two-way street and that both partners must be willing to listen and adapt to build a robust and healthy relationship.

As a speech-language pathologist, I have worked with several children who struggle with selective mutism. Unfortunately, this condition is often misunderstood, and many people do not realize its impact on a child's life.

Selective mutism is a complex disorder that affects a child's ability to speak in certain situations, even though they may be perfectly capable of speaking in others. This condition is not simply shyness or a reluctance to say; it is a natural and severe disorder that can significantly impact a child's social and academic development.

The causes of selective mutism are not fully understood, but it is believed to be related to anxiety and fear. Children with selective mutism may fear social situations, such as school or public places, and feel overwhelmed by the pressure to speak. They may also have experienced trauma or other underlying anxiety disorders contributing to their inability to speak.

When working with children with selective mutism, it is essential to approach treatment gently and patiently. The goal of treatment is to gradually increase the child's comfort level in speaking, so they can communicate more freely in all situations.

One of the most effective treatments for selective mutism is cognitive behavioral therapy (CBT). This therapy helps children identify their fears and anxieties and develop coping strategies. For example, a child may learn relaxation techniques, such as deep breathing or visualization, to help them manage their stress in social situations.

Another important aspect of treatment is socialization. Children with selective mutism may feel isolated and disconnected from their peers, worsening their anxiety. Socialization therapy helps children develop social skills and build relationships with their peers in a safe and supportive environment.

As a speech-language pathologist, my role in treating selective mutism is to help children improve their communication skills and develop strategies for overcoming their anxiety. This may involve working on specific speech and language goals, such as enhancing articulation, expanding vocabulary, and addressing the underlying anxiety causing selective mutism.

Selective mutism is a challenging disorder, but with the proper treatment and support, children can learn to communicate more effectively and overcome their fears.

This disorder is often observed in children and adults. Individuals may consistently fail to speak in social situations even though they can do so in other contexts. Children with ASD who experience SM may find it particularly challenging to communicate with others and express themselves effectively, leading to developmental difficulties.

Selective mutism in children often presents as a consistent failure to speak in social situations such as school or play dates, where the child is expected to interact with others. Children with this condition may communicate effectively at home or with close family members but become silent in unfamiliar social settings. As a result, their ability to build social connections may be affected, and their academic progress may also suffer.

The root causes of selective mutism in children are still not fully understood. However, it is believed to result from the complex interaction of genetic, environmental, and neurodevelopmental factors. Children with ASD who experience SM may be prone to social anxiety, making it challenging to communicate with others. The fear of negative evaluation or social judgment may further exacerbate their symptoms.

Selective mutism in children requires a multidisciplinary approach to treatment. Therapies such as cognitive-behavioral therapy (CBT) and speech therapy can help children overcome their social anxiety and learn to communicate effectively in different social situations. Parents and caregivers can also play a critical role in providing support and creating a supportive environment for the child. In some cases, medication may also be prescribed to manage anxiety symptoms.

SM can significantly impact a child's social, emotional, and academic development. Early identification and appropriate intervention can make a substantial difference in helping children overcome their communication challenges and improve their quality of life.

Some Words of Wisdom for the Parents of Neurodivergent Adolescents

When it comes to parenting a neurodivergent adolescent, there are a few essential things that every parent ought to keep in mind. To begin, it is essential to keep in mind that autism is a disorder that exists on a spectrum. This indicates that no two people who have autism are exactly the same as one another. Therefore, what is effective for one neurodiverse person might not be effective for another.

Second, do not be reluctant to ask for assistance from qualified individuals. There are a great number of therapists and counselors that focus their practices on dealing with adolescents on the autism spectrum and the families of those adolescents. Finally, make sure to retain an open line of communication with your teenager. It is necessary to grasp their perspective by letting them know you are there for them. This may not be a simple task, but it is essential to do so. You can be of great assistance to your teenager who has autism by following these straightforward recommendations and putting them into practice.

Neurodivergence Can be a Strength

When caring for an adolescent who is neurodivergent, it is important to understand the particular strengths that separate them apart from their friends who are neurotypical. There are many ways in which having can be beneficial, despite the fact that the condition presents its own unique set of difficulties in certain areas. People with autism, for instance, have the propensity to be extremely honest and to possess a robust sense of fairness. They frequently have a remarkable capacity for learning and recalling information.

Additionally, autistic people typically have an exceptional capacity for focus and attention to detail in their daily lives. They can build off of these strengths to improve their performance in school and in the occupations they pursue in the future. For instance, if they are trustworthy and have a strong desire to see justice done, they can choose a career as a lawyer or an advocate for social reform. If they are exceptionally smart and have excellent memories, they may pursue careers as physicians or scientists.

There is no upper limit to what a teenager who is neurodivergent is capable of doing in their lifetime. The important thing is to acknowledge each person's distinctive qualities and work to their benefit. They have the potential to accomplish everything they set their minds to if they put in the effort. However, there needs to be some form of control in the age of ease of information and online presence.

Marc Brackett, the Permission to Feel author, mentioned previously, says that 45percent of teenagers are online almost constantly. They spend about six hours a day on social media or surfing the internet; when people spend more time on screens, they have less time to do the things that are important to them, like thinking about their feelings. What further complicates things is that when emotionally immature parents don't know how to handle their children's emotions, they frequently take them personally. They punish their children for feeling undesirable and make them feel ashamed for feeling them instead of helping them deal with them (Brackett, 2019).

The Negative Effects of Social Media on Autistic Teenagers

Social media has more negative than positive elements, no matter who you are. The dangers of sexual grooming, indoctrination, and manipulation are constantly there. Statistics show that approximately 37percent of 12 to 17-year-olds globally have been victims of cyberbullying (Atske, 2022). It is no coincidence that teen suicides have become troublingly frequent in the social media age and that emotional intelligence can be stunted by excessive screen time.

The good news is that autistic teenagers spend less time on social media compared with their neurotypical counterparts. Studies have shown that 13.2 percent of autistic teenagers use social media. It is the responsibility of parents and teachers to explain the dangers of social media to teenagers, including the disconnect from reality. It isn't all bad, though. YouTube, for instance, which isn't based on direct interaction, has some really good channels run by autistic individuals that can be used to develop and understand how others feel emotions. Some of my favorites are as follows:

- The Aspie World www.youtube.com/@TheAspieWorld
- Autism from the Inside www.youtube.com/watch?v=A9nDmiYUSlA
- Yo Samdy Sam www.youtube.com/watch?v=pMx1DnSn-eg

The Significance of Having Many Support Systems Available When One is a Teenager

Autistic teens have access to a wide variety of support networks that can assist them in navigating the difficulties that may arise as they mature. Teenagers who participate in these programs may develop the skills necessary to achieve academic and personal success. Teenagers with autism are able to conquer obstacles and be active members of their communities if they have access to the appropriate support systems, for instance:

- Center for Autism and Related Disorders

    - centerforautism.com

- Key Autism Services

    - www.keyautismservices.com/

- Step Ahead ABA

    - nc.stepaheadaba.com/

Chapter 9

Listen to the Words (or Lack Thereof)

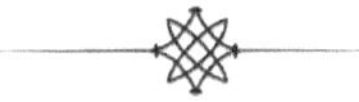

We communicate so that we may be understood, so that our needs can be supported, so that we can ask for directions, so that we can describe, and even so that we can share a memory with someone we care about. As technologies and gadgets that can facilitate alterations to the ways in which we communicate become more widely available, there are now more methods than ever before to communicate. Some people write, some people sign, and some people use tools.

Communication is NOT acquired language, nor is it speech; rather, it is the means by which we attain comprehension as well as the speech that we use. In addition to this, it enables social contact.

There is always a combination of verbal communication, non-verbal communication, and both in every interaction. Our daily interactions consist of approximately 80 percent non-verbal communication and 20 percent verbal communication. This is due to the fact that we communicate with one another through the movements and postures of our bodies, the expressions on our faces, the intonation of our voices, and the noises we make. Non-verbal learning disability, or NVLD, is a condition that affects some people and makes it challenging for them to speak or interact as successfully as others.

Non-Verbal Autism

Statistics show that about 40percent of autistic individuals are completely non-verbal. That leaves a 60% quotient, many of whom are partially verbal and partially non-verbal, which means that understanding your child's communication style is vitally important.

Communication is essential for any person providing care. Speech is the primary mode of communication used by most people and may tell you everything from whether or not your child is hungry to whether or not they are upset. On the other hand, some children who have autism spectrum disorder (ASD) do not speak at all. However, this does not imply that they are unable to communicate or that they are not interested in doing so. People who have ASD still have the same goals as everyone else when it comes to expressing their thoughts and feelings. Still, they do so through gestures, sounds, and other forms of nonverbal communication.

Autism without verbal symptoms is not a recognized diagnostic category. People who are diagnosed with autism spectrum disorder (ASD) and never learn to speak more than a few words are referred to by this subcategory of the disorder. It is estimated that forty percent of those diagnosed with ASD are nonverbal.

The condition known as severe autism, also referred to as level 3 autism, is typically associated with the presence of nonverbal autism. A child may eventually develop the ability to communicate verbally in certain circumstances. New methods of treatment and technological advancements are making it feasible for children who have autism to communicate in various ways, even if they do not speak.

Level 3 autism is typically associated with the presence of nonverbal autism. However, a child may eventually develop the ability to communicate verbally in certain circumstances. In addition, new treatment methods and technological advancements are making it feasible for children who have autism to communicate in various ways, even if they do not speak.

So Then, How Do These Non-Verbal Individuals Communicate?

Many parents of non-speakers can tell you the signs of enthusiasm that a non-speaker is experiencing, as well as the instances that signal sadness, anguish, or frustration. It is more challenging to learn an autistic person's body language because it is not invariably typical of other people's body language. We must refrain from attributing a lack of intelligence or ability to non-speakers just because they do not speak and appear disinterested in connections with others. Non-speakers may not be able to convey that their ear has been hurting for several hours or what they think of the characters in their favorite stories. This is why the exploration of AAC is so important. You may wonder why a child doesn't just point to their ear if they are non-speaking and they are experiencing pain in the ear. We must remember that the neurodivergent mind does not work in the same way as a neurotypical mind. Sometimes those differences do not allow someone to make the connections needed to indicate something like an earache. Sometimes, it could be that their interoceptive sense does not function properly. Sometimes, they are unable to formulate their thoughts into words, so they may not be thinking in language or pictures. Therefore, they cannot come up with a way to indicate ear pain. As a caregiver, we must be highly astute to subtle changes that may occur in the moods and behaviors of non-speaking individuals.

It is worth noting that several non-speaking people do not yet have access to communication. Some parents and family members have exhausted all possible options but have not discovered anything their child can use to communicate in a practical setting. This circumstance can be a heartbreaking experience for both the autistic person and their family. Some people do not have the financial means to investigate alternative approaches. Some people may be unaware of the available choices. Even if their child expresses their affection for them in other ways, the words "I love you" are the only thing that some parents and families want to hear from their child.

"And sometimes, just sometimes, we are comfortable in our silence and not interested in communicating, even if we have a way to communicate" (Mahler, 2020).

Are non-verbal autistic people not physically able to speak, or is it more a choice not to speak? I'm ignorant about this and would like to know more.

"Neither. I've experienced selective mutism a few times. Your ability to form words is just gone. During one episode, even though I couldn't talk, I could still make sounds and answer yes or no questions with "mm hm, mm mm." But even that was hard.

There are all these thoughts in your brain that you want to get out of. But you just can't parse them into words. I've had other episodes where when I talked, it was practically nonsense. The words all jumbled together in my head, trying to make sense of abstract concepts. I'm even confused by the words that come out. I guess it makes sense because autistic brains tend not to have differentiation between hemispheres. Abstract and linear thinking are mixed together.

Neurotypicals can shift between abstract and linear thinking (their default state is linear thinking). It's one or the other thing. Autistic people don't switch hemispheres. The whole brain swings from linear to abstract and areas in between. Abstract thinking is also linked with emotional processing, which makes sense because selective mutism is often triggered by strong emotions.

When it comes to completely nonverbal autistics, I think there's more going on than that. Some of them are able to formulate their thoughts into words using alternative communication devices, writing, sign language, etc. So, they are able to think linearly. They can usually still make sounds. But the ability to formulate words just isn't there.

I was nonverbal until I was four. It took the help of a speech therapist to get me to talk. Some autistic people have no speech delays. Some can overcome speech issues with help. Some never do. The inability to speak has nothing to do with intelligence or physical issues. It's a processing error. Either internally (abstract thought process) or in networking (the speech center of the brain's control over the mouth)" (Grimm, n.d.).

www.quora.com/Can-someone-who-isnt-autistic-go-non-verbal

Visual Tools

Spoken language can prove challenging to children, even if they are not non-speaking communicators. Remember that putting words into meaning during a conversation or describing how a situation made a child feel is often something that doesn't come easily. The story of Aiden and describing an occurrence as his "brain being on crack" in chapter 1 is a good example of this. He was unable to ask to be excused because he didn't have the words. Aiden had never been taught the words to use to make an exit in those circumstances, as well as the words necessary to describe what he was experiencing. As I said, I spent the session that followed giving Aiden the words and the following visual tools are ones that can help in preparing autistic children for similar experiences.

Creating Gantt Charts

These can be found online, but to briefly explain, Gantt charts show activities against time. Kind of like a bar chart with time vertically and the task (a science class, let's say) horizontally. This provides a visual representation of a schedule. You can access all the information on Gantt.com.

Social Stories

Carol Gray, a multiple award-winning autism consultant, is responsible for the creation of Carol Gray Social Stories ©. In 1989, Carol began writing stories for her autistic students within the Michigan-based Jenison Public School Group and noted great results in coping with day-to-day life, including a vast array of interactions.

Unplanned events can happen and may be challenging to deal with. Preparing your child for the unexpected via social stories can be an excellent tool to increase communication and decrease anxiety.

Stories and drawings can be simple but powerful. You don't have to be an artist to write a social story for your child.

Go right ahead and make stick figures and a simple bus to tell a story about how sometimes people get sick. For example, the usual driver is sick today, so Ms. Holly is helping drive the children on the school bus until Ms. Brenda feels better. When Ms. Brenda is better, she will drive the bus again.

Timers

I'm sure your first thought was "hourglass," and if so, you would be correct. You could also use a "Time Timer," which is a battery-operated clock-type machine that represents time in one-hour passages. The website, www.timetimer.com/, offers reasonably priced timers and a range of other time-keeping products.

Picture Cards

Just like neurotypicals respond to picture cards, autistic children do the same. Cast your mind back to the picture of the cat, with the word "cat" written below it. There are apps and devices that offer digital picture cards, but I prefer the old-school type of cards!

Video-Based Teaching

TV can be a great teacher as long as the material is educational but also enjoyable for the child. Learning when it is appropriate to use certain phrases and respond to social cues can be conveyed well by video. Internalization of content by repetition, as well as the combination of verbal and visual content, can be attributed to this type of learning.

Video Modeling

The idea of video modeling is to show rather than tell, and it involves two facets. Firstly, there are specifically acted videos, and secondly, there are videos made in class, therapy, or at the home of the child and their behaviors. This teaching technique focuses on body language and facial expressions. As before, children can have trouble identifying when empathy is required, and the advantage that video modeling has over static content is that videos are more realistic in terms of showing what others are feeling. The same applies to the "unwritten" social rules that are kind of "just there" in society, which are better displayed via video, as opposed to static images.

Video Previews

If you go to a theme park or a zoo, to use an example, there are often induction-type videos that are shown to school groups as preparation for the upcoming experience. The same can be applied in therapy, at school, or at home for the same preparatory purposes.

Emotional Intelligence and Learning

Verywellmind.com defines emotional intelligence as "the ability to perceive, interpret, demonstrate, control, evaluate, and use emotions to communicate with and relate to others effectively and constructively."

The above can be read as a list of skills that children lack, but fortunately, emotional intelligence can be taught, although it remains difficult to learn. The premise is based on the Theory of Mind, which hypothesizes that the better you are at imagining or seeing the world from another person's perspective, the better you are at displaying emotional intelligence (The Family Guidance and Therapy Center, 2022). But before we get to that point, it is important to educate our children about their own emotions. It is difficult to learn emotional intelligence without the foundation of the basics of emotions and how they manifest on a child-to-child basis. As a parent, there are a few things you can do to achieve this.

Acknowledge and Label

If your child has a meltdown, there is little that you can do at the time. However, at a later stage, you can have a question-and-answer session, where you allow your child to describe how they felt. From that point, you can attach a label to the emotion. There are several benefits for the child, including developing the ability to identify AND name the emotions in others.

Encourage Expression of Emotions

Can you imagine if we all suppressed our emotions? The world would be a melting pot ready to explode. Different emotions are displayed differently by different people, and we need to convey to our children that it is okay to experience the feelings they are having. The next step is to suggest and give examples of alternative outlets, as well as social situations during which one should not act on an emotion. It is "socially inappropriate" to get angry and punch someone in the face, but many adults do it anyway. The point is that it can be very difficult to refrain from acting on a negative emotion, and children must be made aware of the difficulty. Acceptance of emotions and feelings, leading to regulation, is the end goal. Don't forget to let your child know that they are not being judged and must not judge themselves.

Listen

We all sometimes need someone to just listen, free of judgment, criticism, and distraction; it helps us to let go of things and move on. Teachers, therapists, and parents need to create a non-judgmental atmosphere and pay 100percent attention to what the child wants to say. There doesn't need to be a set time for this, but making observations and basing questions on the observations can encourage a child to talk. Here are a few suggestions on how to use language correctly to facilitate an environment where you become a listener (as a parent):

- It looks like something is bothering you. You know that's okay, right? I'm here if you'd like to talk about it, but it's completely fine if you don't.

- Some days I get frustrated at work. Do you ever get frustrated?

- You seem really happy! Would you like to tell me about things that make you feel happy?

The third example is probably the easiest, but it's all about making the child feel comfortable talking, knowing that you will listen without distraction.

Roleplay and Problem-Solving

Feelings and emotions can be better understood through roleplay, which leads to problem-solving in the sense of dealing with emotions. Sharing is a good example, and can be addressed through a role-play exercise where you, as a parent, act like you have a toy that you don't want to share. Your child can be given the role of asking if they can play with your toy, and you can explain that the right thing to do is to say "Yes," and encourage sharing.

Now What?

Well, you now have the knowledge, understanding, methods, and a manual, in the form of this book, to do the best you can do to give your child the words and the actions (in the case of non-verbal autism). All these methods create greater knowledge and understanding, which leads to the identification of similar emotions within others, and emotional intelligence is allowed to develop.

Conclusion

It would be safe to say that if you have reached this point, then you are in a more educated position on children and the importance of giving them words. Below is a consolidated recap that can be used as a set of reference points to go back to areas that were particularly informative and that you, the reader, have identified with.

Children can struggle to find the words to express their feelings, and a case in point is that of Aiden and the sensory overload that he experienced but was unable to react verbally at the time. Don't forget that naming emotions is useful in creating understanding. If a child expresses anger without understanding what the emotion actually is but is taught what it is through roleplay and assigning the correct word, then steps are being taken to give the words to that child.

As we now know, there are eight senses as opposed to five, and the processing of sensory information either prevents children from or encourages them to adapt to their environments. Take note of the story of Jayden in chapter two and how his sensory overload created dysregulation. Basically, Jayden was bombarded by sensory unpleasantness from the moment that he woke up until he became so dysregulated that he punched another child at his school.

Although difficult to control, there are sensory devices that can be used to mitigate dysregulation. For example, lava lamps for sight sensitivity or weighted blankets for touch seekers. When used in conjunction with exercises, such as swimming or bike riding, for improved spatial awareness of proprioception deficiency or obstacle courses for interoception difficulties.

Just like sense, there are eight components to communication, very briefly summarized below:

- Source: Choosing the correct selection of words to convey meaning.

- Message: Conveying the meaning via the selected words/even actions.

- Channel: Talking, writing, even drawing.

- Receiver: The person receiving and interpreting the message.

- Feedback: Display of how accurately the message has been interpreted.

- Environment: The environment in which you communicate.

- Context: Casual context, such as on the beach, or less casual, say during therapy.

- Interference: Exterior factors such as background noise or uncomfortable lighting.

On the subject of learning, there are many methods, some of which overlap. However, certain categories are commonly acknowledged. Visual or spatial learners benefit from flashcards, schedules, sketching, and videos. Auditory exercises include using music or filmed lectures to teach. These are suited to autistic listeners. Role play and group discussion suit linguistic learners best, especially involving reading and writing. In addition, you get social, physical, natural, and logical learners, as explained in chapter three.

Following on from the different types of learning, there are also language processing differences. Because children are often more literal than adults, they often gravitate towards analytical language processing, which is a logical breaking down of the language. Then you have Gestalt language processing, where the meaning of the language is discerned as a whole, meaning that there is less focus on every single word.

Echolalia, being the repetition of words or sentences heard from others, can be related to both types of language processing and in certain instances, can be problematic. As I have mentioned, repetition is the basis for learning anything. However, when it is unfounded or excessive, then speech therapy should be considered. Explaining visual and verbal cues, as well as positive reinforcement, are also means to treat echolalia.

All children deserve to have access to education, but it isn't always that easy because of alternative needs. The Individuals with Disabilities Education Act (IDEA) is the legislation that facilitates free education appropriate to children with disabilities. Even though autism is not a disability, it falls under the auspices of the act, which is a good thing in that it upholds the rights of autistic children to receive an appropriate education. The downside is that sensory integration therapy is not always seen as educationally relevant. However, there does seem to be a shift away from this mindset, and it is books like this that need to create awareness on the subject to assist in this mindset change.

Broadly speaking, there are several ways to promote learning in the visual sense. Some examples are Gantt charts, picture cards, and video-based teaching, as explored in chapter six. The use of social stories under the umbrella of the Carol Gray Social Stories © brand has proven successful in teaching autistic children how to cope in situations that are the same or similar to what they have read or listened to. Emotional intelligence is a set of skills that can be honed via social stories and can be explained as part of the theory of mind. In short, when children can see, interpret and understand another person's point of view, then they can identify with that person in an emotionally intelligent way.

In terms of understanding, children should be taught how to acknowledge an emotion, put a name to it, and not be ashamed to display that emotion, BUT not in ways that are harmful to others. We can achieve this by listening to what our children have to say through open-ended questions and giving them the option to start a discussion or not. Initiating these conversations should be done in a comfortable environment, non-intrusively and non-judgmentally.

Referring back to Marc Brackett's book, *Permission to Feel*, there are judgmental parents out there. Don't be one! Also, don't be a parent that allows free reign in terms of access to social media. The statistics, as discussed in chapter six, are alarming, and it is a parental duty to explain the dangers of social media to your children, autistic or not. Having said that, there are positives and learning facilities through the YouTube channels that I mentioned, among others. Either way, you need to be proactive and not reactive.

In chapter seven, we looked at the way in which children are influenced by the experiences that happen at home. Apart from the constant love and support that parents of autistic children (all children) need to provide, the home can be set up in such a way as to create a comfortable environment. This involves catering to sensory needs in such a way as to allow your child to be him or herself. Assistance in understanding and encouraging communication, verbal or otherwise, that meets the needs of your child goes a long way to establishing that comfort. There will undoubtedly be challenges and tough days, but you, as a parent, need to be kind to yourself when you can. We all need emotional support at times, so don't be hesitant to reach out when you need it, and don't be afraid to break out of the identity mold as the parent of an autistic child.

Find time for the things you love. Whether you enjoy exercising, swimming, reading, or whatever, allow yourself to enjoy those activities. As I recommended and still do, take a look into CBT and Mindfulness as escapes from the rigors of day-to-day life. Don't forget the stigma around autistic children, and make an effort to spread awareness in your own way, no matter how small. Remember you are not alone and know that you can take solace in the words of other parents from the raisingchildren.net.au video in chapter seven.

There is a lot to learn from my realizations while watching *American Tragedy*, but as I said, it reinforced what I already knew. The major takeaway is that the most effective approaches for social and emotional learning should be integrated into school curriculums and provide skill building across all grade levels to reach all children. This lends itself to the best social and emotional learning efforts as proactive, not reactive.

On the topic of proactivity, another point to consider is the transition from childhood through puberty, which is tough for any child. However, autistic children may have big struggles coping with the biological changes. Neurodivergent girls have been noted to have trouble interacting socially with neurotypical girls during puberty, with adverse effects on mental health. This is not to say that boys find it any easier, but the proactive endeavors to brace children for puberty will only do them favors. You want your child to gain some form of independence, which is facilitated by teaching social skills, including masking, and why it should be avoided.

It is a good idea to anticipate changes and develop support systems, in addition to showing your child that neurodivergence means many strengths through the teenage years and into adulthood, which is a great self-esteem booster. Educating children on unhealthy relationships with social media, as well as the good that can come of social media, in preparation for when your child takes an interest, can prevent cyberbullying and the other evils of the internet. The three YouTube channels that I listed at the end of chapter 8 are worth looking at. Firstly, as a parent, and then with your child as a parent/teacher.

I am confident that you'll be able to give your children the words, but if not, you will be able to give them the feelings and the means to self-expression. So, although words are important, the overriding importance is communication. On that note, I would like to leave you with a quote from author Peter Drucker:

The most important part about communication is to hear what is not being said.

Sometimes, we need to hear what our children are not saying so that we can give them the words!

References

Alhujaili, N., Platt, E., Khalid-Khan, S., & Groll, D. (2022). Comparison of social media use among adolescents with autism spectrum disorder and non-ASD adolescents. *Adolescent health, medicine and therapeutics*, Volume 13, 15–21. https://doi.org/10.2147/ahmt.s344591

Atske, Sara. (2022, December 15). *Teens and cyberbullying 2022.* www.pewresearch.org/internet/2022/12/15/teens-and-cyberbullying-2022/

Beck, C. (2022, December 06). *Understanding sensory dysregulation.* https://www.theottoolbox.com/understanding-sensory-dysregulation/

Better health. (2014). *Nervous system.* Vic.gov.au. https://www.betterhealth.vic.gov.au/health/conditionsandtreatments/nervous-system

Brennan, D. (2021, October 25). *What is echolalia?* https://www.webmd.com/parenting/what-is-echolalia

Cherry, K. (2022, November 7). *What is emotional intelligence?* Verywell Mind. https://www.verywellmind.com/what-is-emotional-intelligence-2795423

Children & autism: Videos. (n.d.). Raising Children Network. Retrieved April 25, 2023, from http://raisingchildren.net.au/autism/children-autism-videos

Delano, C. (2021, July 28). *Benefits of early intervention speech therapy.* Autism Parenting Magazine. https://www.autismparentingmagazine.com/early-intervention-speech-therapy/

Delano, C. (2022, February 18). *Benefits of sign language for autism.* https://www.autismparentingmagazine.com/autistic-child-sign-language/

Echolalia and its role in gestalt language acquisition. (n.d.). American Speech-Language-Hearing Association. https://www.asha.org/Practice-Portal/Clinical-Topics/Autism/Echolalia-and-Its-Role-in-Gestalt-Language-Acquisition/

Gordon, S. (2022, November). *What is hyperlexia?* Verywell Family. https://www.verywellfamily.com/hyperlexia-signs-diagnosis-and-treatment-5206172

Gray, C. (2015). *Social stories.* Carol Gray - Social Stories. https://carolgraysocialstories.com/about-2/carol-gray/

Guidance, T. F., & Center, T. (2022, January 21). *Do autistic people have emotional intelligence?* Familyguidanceandtherapy.com.

https://familyguidanceandtherapy.com/do-autistic-individuals-have-emotional-intelligence/

A guide to the individualized education program office of special education and rehabilitative services U.S. department of education. (2000). https://www2.ed.gov/parents/needs/speced/iepguide/iepguide.pdf

Helping kids understand the connection between feelings and moods. (n.d.). Fit.sanfordhealth.org. https://fit.sanfordhealth.org/units/u2-k2-helping-kids-manage-feelings-and-emotions/u2l1-k2-helping-kids-understand-the-connection-between-feelings-and-moods

Home. (n.d.). Key Autism Services. http://www.keyautismservices.com

Home. (n.d.-b). Center for Autism and Related Disorders (CARD®). http://centerforautism.com

Hyperlexia: What is it, and how can I support a hyperlexic learner? (2023). Twinkl.com. http://www.twinkl.com/blog/hyperlexia-what-is-it-and-how-can-i-support-a-hyperlexic-learner

Kuypers, L. (2014, December). *Emotional self regulation | senses.* Scribd. https://www.scribd.com/doc/312176471/leah-kuypers-handouts-zones-of-regulation?utm_medium=cpc&utm_source=google_pmax&utm_campaign=3Q_Google_PerformanceMax_RoW&utm_term=&utm_device=c&gclid=CjwKCAjw9J2iBhBPEiwAErwpeaE3qHq5WUEmZT-7WyFYFB_m2dYllJvuTh-FXu-zcFtK4OzWB2TF7BoCK8UQAvD_BwE#

Kuypers, L. (2011). *The zones of regulation: A concept to foster self-regulation & emotional control.* The Zones of Regulation. https://zonesofregulation.com/index.html

Joiya, S.. (2018, November 20). *5 steps to emotional intelligence.* Autism Point. https://autismpoint.com/5-steps-to-emotional-intelligence/

Lovering, N. (2016, October 14). *Autism and logical thinking: What to know.* Psych Central. https://psychcentral.com/autism/why-people-with-autism-are-more-logical

Magnuson, K. M., & Constantino, J. N. (2011). Characterization of depression in children with autism spectrum disorders. *Journal of Developmental & Behavioral Pediatrics*, 32(4), 332–340. https://doi.org/10.1097/dbp.0b013e318213f56c

Mahler, J. (n.d.). https://www.quora.com/profile/Jess-Burde-Mahler

Mayo Clinic. (2019, September 17). *Selective serotonin reuptake inhibitors (ssris)*. Mayo Clinic; Mayo Clinic. https://www.mayoclinic.org/diseases-conditions/depression/in-depth/ssris/art-20044825

Merriam-Webster. (n.d.). *Savant definition & meaning*. https://www.merriam-webster.com/dictionary/savant

The most interesting facts about the human nervous system. (n.d.). BYJUS. https://byjus.com/biology/facts-about-nervous-system/

OSMD. (2016, June 10). *4 ways that music and mathematics are related*. OSMD. https://www.omahaschoolofmusicanddance.com/our-blog/4-ways-that-music-and-mathematics-are-related/

Psychology professor jobs. (n.d.). Recruit.net. https://www.recruit.net/job/professor-psychology-jobs/4A0674D7151458CC

Rabbit, M. (2022, December 17). *Marc brackett, founder and director of the yale center for emotional intelligence, says doing these 3 things can help you feel safe and seen during the holidays*. The Sunday Paper PLUS. https://www.mariashriversundaypaper.com/marc-brackett-founder-and-director-of-the-yale-center-for-emotional-intelligence-says-doing-these-3-things-can-help-you-feel-safe-and-seen-during-the-holidays/

Rudy, L. (2021, June 14). *7 visual tools that can help people with autism learn and thrive*. Verywell Health. https://www.verywellhealth.com/visual-thinking-and-autism-5119992#:~:text=Visualspercent20makepercent20itpercent20easierpercent20for

Slate, K. (2022, December 11). *6 signs of insecurity in A relationship you should never ignore*. Bonobology. https://bonobologyzz.pages.dev/posts/6-signs-of-insecurity-in-a-relationship-you-should-never-ignore/

Socialthinking - Social thinking. (n.d.). Socialthinking.com. https://www.socialthinking.com/Speakerpercent20Details?name=Leah+Kuyperspercent2C+Guest+Speaker#:~:text=Leahpercent20Kuyperspercent20ispercent20anpercent20OT

Step ahead ABA therapy | applied behavior analysis therapy at home. (n.d.). Step Ahead ABA North Carolina. Retrieved April 25, 2023, from http://nc.stepaheadaba.com

Team, C. (2022, December 13). *Analytic vs gestalt language processing.* Cutting Edge Therapy. https://cuttingedgepediatrictherapy.com/2022/12/analytic-vs-Gestalt-language-processing

Team, T. (2020, October 22). *How to get an early intervention evaluation.* Www.understood.org. https://www.understood.org/en/articles/how-to-request-an-early-intervention-evaluation

U.S. Department of Education. (2023). *Individuals with disabilities education act.* Ed.gov. https://sites.ed.gov/idea/about-idea

Villegas, T. (2022, October 5). *10 videos that tell the stories of people who use augmentative and alternative communication (AAC).* Think Inclusive. http://www.thinkinclusive.us/post/videos-films-augmentative-alternative-communication

Weiss. (2017, August 3). *York U study finds benefits for parents who participate in therapy with autistic children.* Research & Innovation. https://www.yorku.ca/research/category/news/2017/08/york-u-study-finds-benefits-for-parents-who-participate-in-therapy-with-autistic-children/

What makes autistic people so good at math? (2017, July 25). Www.appliedbehavioranalysisedu.org. https://www.appliedbehavioranalysisedu.org/

what-makes-autistic-people-so-good-at-math/#:~:text=Lookingpercent20atpercent20 apercent20grouppercent20of

Yacoub, A. (2022, May 2). *What it Means to be neurodiversity affirming* | TherapyWorks. Therapyworks.com. https://therapyworks.com/blog/child-development/what-it-means-to-be-neurodiversity-affirming